MONICA CONNELL

Against a Peacock Sky

VIKING

VIKING

Published by the Penguin Group
Penguin Books Ltd, 27 Wrights Lane, London W8 5TZ, England
Viking Penguin, a division of Penguin Books USA Inc.
375 Hudson Street, New York, New York 10014, USA
Penguin Books Australia Ltd, Ringwood, Victoria, Australia
Penguin Books Canada Ltd, 2801 John Street, Markham, Ontario, Canada L3R 1B4
Penguin Books (NZ) Ltd, 182–190 Wairau Road, Auckland 10, New Zealand

Penguin Books Ltd, Registered Offices: Harmondsworth, Middlesex, England

First published 1991
1 3 5 7 9 10 8 6 4 2

Printed in Great Britain by Butler & Tanner Ltd, Frome and London
Set in $10\frac{1}{2}/13\frac{1}{2}$ pt Lasercomp Photina

A CIP catalogue record for this book is available from the British Library

ISBN 0-670-834637

Library of Congress Catalog Card Number: 90–71284

For Jaktu, Bānchu, Lākśmi, Sauni, Hira Lāl,
Biḍa, Jakali, Śaṅkar, Kālo, Nara Bahādur
and Bātuli

CONTENTS

LIST OF PLATES

ACKNOWLEDGEMENTS

I'm grateful to the Northern Ireland Department of Education, who financed my research in Nepal. For his help during the period of research, I'm indebted to Gabriel Campbell, especially for the use of myths and quotations, without which the book would be infinitely less colourful. Thanks, too, to four Jumla schoolteachers: Ṭasi Bahādur Buṛa, Nara Bahādur Buṛa, Keśāb Mahat and Chandan Rokāya, who patiently answered innumerable questions; and especially to Keśāb Mahat for his help with transcribing and translating stories and songs.

For their support during the writing of the book, I'm indebted to many friends and relatives, but in particular to Hanna Connell; to Chris Sheppard for his determination to see the manuscript published; to Debbie Taylor and Myra Connell, who read several drafts of each story and whose criticism was both sensitive and thorough; and to Myra Connell and Mark Chamberlain for their belief in me, which has meant more than I can say.

Very special thanks are due to Dieter Klein, my agent, and to Tessa Strickland, former commissioning editor at Penguin. Thanks also to Clare Alexander, publishing director, and to Jennifer Munka, copy editor.

But my greatest debt is to the people of Talphi, especially the family with whom we lived; and to Peter Barker, who shared so many experiences with me, and whose photographs tell a similar story to my own in a very different way. *Against a Peacock Sky* is their book as much as mine.

PRONUNCIATION GUIDE

For any readers who are interested, I include notes on the pronunciation of Nepāli words.

VOWELS

a   Varies between *u* in b*u*t and *o* in n*o*t
ā   Like *a* in f*a*ther
i, ī   Both pronounced like *i* in French l*i*t
u, ū   Both pronounced like *ou* in French c*ou*p
o   Like *ô* in French t*ô*t
ai   Diphthong, with a pronounced like *a* in *a*rise and i like *y* in cit*y*
au   Diphthong, with a pronounced like *a* in *a*rise and u like *u* in p*u*t
ṅ   Indicates that the preceding vowel is nasalized, as in French sa*ng*, *en*, ci*nq*, mo*nt*, lu*nd*i

CONSONANTS

d   Like *d* in French *d*it
ḍ   Like *d* in *d*ay
h   On its own it is hardly pronounced. Following a consonant, it indicates that *that* consonant is aspirated, or pronounced with a strong exhalation of breath (an exception to this is ch which is unaspirated [pronounced like the ty sound at the beginning of tutor] and its aspirated counterpart, chh [pronounced like the *ch* in *ch*ange])
j   Like *j* in French *j*eune
ph   Like *f*, but pronounced without upper teeth touching lip
r   Like *r* in Italian Ma*r*ia
ṛ   Very similar to ḍ
ṣ   Usually like *s* in *s*ing
ś   Like *sh* in *sh*ip
t   Like *t* in French *t*ôt
ṭ   Like *t* in *t*ame
w   Hardly pronounced

All Nepāli words are in italics and are in the Glossary.

INTRODUCTION

FOR A LONG TIME I'D EXPECTED TO GO ALONE TO NEPAL TO DO THE field-work for my Ph.D. in social anthropology so, when Peter decided to come with me as photographer, research assistant, partner, I was delighted. The apprehension that I'd felt about being on my own in a remote place now turned into the healthy anticipation of adventure: we started going to Nepāli classes at the School of Oriental and African Studies in London; we scrutinized maps and guide books; we drew up lists and went shopping for things we would need.

At that time we knew roughly which part of the country we'd go to, although not which particular village. The only real requirement was that it should be a Hindu, Nepāli-speaking community. Apart from this, like most anthropologists I imagined being somewhere remote. I was romantic about field-work to the extent that I wanted to immerse myself in a traditional culture, one that was still relatively untainted by modern and Western influences. I was also keen to be somewhere that hadn't already been overrun by anthropologists – I wanted a patch of my own.

From the reading I had done, Jumla District, in the northwestern Himalayan foothills, seemed to be the obvious choice. Jumla Bazaar, the District centre, is about ten days' walk from the nearest motorable road, and although there has been a small airport with twice-weekly flights to and from Kathmandu since the 1960s, I reasoned that this would have little bearing on the lives of people one or two days' walk away.

As to other anthropologists: from what I could gather there hadn't been many. The few who had worked there for any length of time had been researching high-caste Hindus – Brahmans, Chhetris and Ṭhakuris. Reading their work, I came across numerous references to a group of people that no one had studied in

3

depth – the *matawāli* Chhetris*. According to their clan names *matawāli* Chetris are high-caste Hindus, yet in significant ways their culture and religion belie this identity, and have led anthropologists to speculate that they could once have been a tribal people who migrated into the area and, over the years, assimilated with the surrounding Hindu culture. Although *matawāli* Chhetri communities are scattered throughout the District, there is apparently one valley – the Chaudabis Dāra – where they are virtually the only inhabitants (apart from a few Ḍum† or Untouchable communities). Without a doubt, this was where I wanted to go.

Although this question of the *matawāli* Chetri identity intrigued me, I didn't want to have an agenda. I was cynical enough, even in those early days, to be warned by the anthropologist who had spent ten years studying the language and culture of a tribe and then, on his first day in the field, found them speaking English, drinking Coca-Cola and dancing to American pop music on the radio. I wanted to go there, learn and document as much as possible, and then write my thesis on whatever seemed significant – in whatever way appropriate.

Both in England and, later, in Kathmandu people warned us against working in Jumla. Their main reason was its relative inaccessibility. Although flights were regular in the spring and autumn, they stopped completely during the monsoon – from the end of June until the beginning of October – and were unpredictable during the winter when there was likely to be snow. In practical terms this meant that if there was an emergency, such as either of us being taken ill, we might have difficulty getting out. There were other reasons too. Many Kathmandu Nepalis regarded Jumla as a backwater. They told us it was bitterly cold, 'under-developed', and that the people – unused to foreigners –

---

*'*Matawāli*' means alcohol-drinking. Most high-caste Hindus in Jumla (including orthodox Chhetris) don't drink alcohol because it is defiling. The term is only used by anthropologists, not by the people themselves.

†The main Ḍum castes in the area are *Damāi* – tailors (and musicians), *Sārki* – leatherworkers, and *Kāmi* – blacksmiths.

would be suspicious, inhospitable and probably hostile.

We thought about this and about Jumla having been declared a 'food-deficit zone' the previous year. We dreaded being an extra burden on scant resources. Nevertheless, we still wanted to go.

From the time we arrived in Kathmandu, it took four months for my research proposal to be approved by Tribhuvan University and for our visas to be subsequently granted. While we were waiting, I continued to go to Nepāli classes, and I spent some time tracking down and reading relevant articles and books. I also met other anthropologists who'd worked in Jumla, including Gabriel Campbell who was unusually generous with his experience and knowledge, and whose thesis* I would consult over and over during the early days of my field-work, when Jumla could just as well have been Mars.

We otherwise filled in the days by gathering things we would need. Some of these we'd brought with us from England: a tape-recorder and blank tapes (for recording myths, songs and possibly interviews), a torch, batteries, a year's supply of film, basic medical supplies, a few 'indispensable' books. Others we collected in Kathmandu: down-jackets, sleeping-bags and walking boots (from the many second-hand trekking shops); cooking pots and pans; tea, coffee, spices, oil, candles – any number of small things that can't be bought or are very expensive in Jumla Bazaar.

But it was really an impossible task, equipping ourselves for a place we knew nothing about. Some of the things that we took (our down-jackets, pressure-cooker, thermos flask) we were grateful for. On the whole, though, I felt that most luxuries created a bad atmosphere – resentment on the part of the people we lived with, and guilt combined with fear of theft on ours. We never regretted not taking a radio; it would undoubtedly have attracted crowds of people (there were one or two radios in the village, but

---

*Gabriel Campbell, 'Consultations with Himalayan Gods: A Study of Oracular Religion and Alternative Values in Hindu Jumla', unpublished Ph.D. thesis, Columbia University, 1978.

most of the time they were without batteries). Anyway, it seemed a rare privilege to be totally out of touch with the rest of the world for such long stretches of time.

We flew to Jumla in a fourteen-seater Twin Otter. Gaining height over Kathmandu City, we looked down on to streets of tall brick houses with strings of chillies hanging drying from the upper windows, temples with tiered pagoda roofs, the hustle and bustle of people and cars. Beyond the city was the green bowl of Kathmandu valley, rich and luxuriant throughout the year. Beyond that, barren brown hills, empty terraces from which the crops had already been harvested, houses clustered on hillsides in tiny cramped villages miles from anywhere. For a while we skirted the high mountain ranges of Annapurna and Daulaghiri, a huge uninhabited world of glistening snow and ice. Then, immediately, we dropped into the narrow valley that was Jumla.

We stayed in the small hotel in Jumla Bazaar. The owner Gaya Prasād, who sadly died during the course of our field-work, took us on an elaborate tour, pointing out the post office, the bank, the military barracks, the police station, the hospital, the unused family planning clinic and the tea shops; the Trade School run by the United Mission; the posts that had been erected to carry hydroelectricity and the trenches dug for drainage (neither project was completed during our time there). Afterwards, he took us to one of the Tibetan *chang* (rice-beer) shops – a precedent for the many happy times we would later spend with him.

We stayed in the Bazaar for four days. Then on the fifth morning, taking only our sleeping bags, we set out to look for a village where we could live and work – Gaya Prasād had suggested Talphi, one of the biggest villages in the Chaudabis valley, and a day's walk away.

If we hadn't been distracted with nerves, it would have been a beautiful walk. We followed the Tila River out of the Bazaar past the airstrip, and then branched off to the north-east, joining the Chaudabis valley. The river was broad and full, churning white and frothy in places, then billowing as smoothly as green silk. At one point we crossed over a wooden bridge with carved figures on each of its four corners, and then climbed high into the vivid reds and yellows of a deciduous wood.

Each time the valley broadened out there was a settlement; we passed first of all through the fields, where people who were working called out to us, asking us where we were going, then through the outskirts of the village. The houses were big, made of stone and mud, with flat roofs where sheaves of grain were drying. Some of them were joined together in terraces; others that were separate were built as closely as possible to take up as little of the flat cultivable land as was necessary.

Just outside one of these villages we came across a small shrine by the side of the path; a thornbush with red and white streamers tied to it and below, on the ground, the signs of a sacrifice – splashes of blood and a handful of feathers. I felt excited at the prospect of coming to understand the religion and the gods and goddesses associated with these shrines. And looking round at the endless mountains with their thick spread of pine forest – now rare in so much of Nepal – I was convinced that we'd made the right choice in coming to Jumla.

The valley opened into the broadest stretch of flat land we'd seen. And there, tucked in close to the valley wall, was Talphi.

As soon as we were inside the village I felt a rush of panic. The paths were littered with heaps of excrement, and the houses were very close together, so there was a sense of being trapped, with people shouting and staring from all sides. A pack of dogs ran after us, barking and snarling, and we had to stop and fend them off with stones.

As we were walking on, a group of men sitting on one of the first roofs called out to us. I shouted back, asking if we could join them. We climbed up the notched-pole ladder and sat down on the rug that one of the men had spread out for us. Peter passed round his cigarettes.

Within seconds a crowd of people had gathered round us.

Everyone was staring. Some of the children came right up close with their faces poised in front of ours, brown eyes riveted without a trace of shyness or embarrassment. Some of them reached out to touch our hair or skin. A group of slightly older boys stood behind them, commenting and giggling, and I heard one young woman teasingly telling her baby that if he wasn't good the foreigners would take him away.

We passed round the cigarettes again. A man was trying to say something to us, but we didn't understand the local dialect. Other men joined in, shouting the same question louder and louder, patient and smiling at first, then growing increasingly frustrated. At last, when we understood, our mutual relief seemed for an instant to bring us closer together. They wanted to know what we were doing here. I had prepared the answer to this question before. I said that in our schools we learn about foreign countries. We wanted to learn about life here so we could write a book about it, and tell other people at home. I added that we'd very much like to stay in Talphi for at least six months, and did they think that would be possible?

While I was speaking everyone listened in silence. My voice sounded strange and small and I couldn't tell if my Kathmandu Nepāli made sense or not. I felt as though I was at an inquisition; the sun was hot and bright, glaring into my eyes and dazzling me and I was squinting up into rows and rows of blackened faces and bodies clothed in filthy tatters.

When I'd finished talking there was a buzz of voices; everyone trying to interpret what I'd said or to comment on it – whether objecting or sympathizing I couldn't tell. After a while one of the men said there was nowhere for us to stay in Talphi. When I asked about other villages nearby, he said he didn't think so.

Soon afterwards when we were standing up, about to leave, a man brought a little girl to the front of the crowd and showed her to us. He said she was four years old; she looked about two. I don't know what was the matter with her, apart from malnutrition, but I knew that she was dying. Her father asked if we had any medicine. There was something in the way he held her, in the way her sleeping body nestled in his arms, that made me want to choke. I said we didn't; he'd have to take her to the hospital. He looked at me as though I'd suggested that he take her to the moon.

We walked on through the village, past the *Ḍum* quarter, throwing stones at dogs. At last, when we were out in the open country, we sat under the shade of a walnut tree. I felt horrified, appalled (and certainly not for the last time) by the sheer arrogance of anthropology.

We sat under the tree for a long time. It was soothing to watch the autumn leaves fluttering to the ground one by one when their time had come. Eventually, we began to think about what we were going to do. The important question now seemed to be not where we would spend the next six months, but where we would spend this one night. Although the October sun was hot, the nights were cold and frosty. In the end we decided to set out back towards the Bazaar, and if night fell before we got there, we could ask to stay in one of the villages along the way. It wasn't a decision either of us was proud of. We knew from the rough map we'd brought from Kathmandu that Talphi was one of a cluster of villages. And we knew that some time we'd have to come back and try them all.

We didn't move from under the tree. Half an hour must have passed. Then, as if from nowhere, two boys (Sigarup and Nara) came running over and told us that their father (Kalchu) had said we could stay with them for six months.

Several hours later, at Kalchu's house, we began to relax. The sun had set and it was getting cold. All the people who'd been so curious about us since we arrived had gone home. We sat outside until it was almost dark. As we watched the village unwinding for the night, everything suddenly seemed reassuringly familiar: people coming back from the fields, the cows and sheep being driven in, the lowing and bleating, the animal smells and the rustle of fresh straw. It could have been a farming community anywhere in the world, at any time in history.

When it was completely dark, we went inside and sat around the fire with Kalchu's family. Again, as we ate our wheat *rotis* and warm milk, I suddenly felt the strangeness of the situation dissolve. We were united by the need to eat and our pleasure in the food – the farmer and the traveller, the host and the guest, the shared need for a warm home at the end of a long day. After we'd eaten, we unpacked our sleeping bags and Kalchu fetched some blankets, and everyone settled down to sleep around the fire.

We left early the next morning, thanking them, and saying we'd be back as soon as possible.

Kalchu's house was divided into three sections. Until the previous year all three had been occupied: by Kalchu and his two younger brothers and their wives and children, and the wives of the sons who were married. Until the year before that, Kalchu's father had lived in the same section that he did. We were able to move into an empty section because the youngest brother had decided to leave and build a small house of his own.

We had two rooms; the outer one had been used only in the monsoon, when it was pleasantly cool because the two outside walls consisted of an open wood frame that was partially plastered over with mud. When we moved in, Kalchu filled in the remaining gaps. This made a room that was rare, if not unique, in the village and suited us well. The fact that the walls were not made of stone meant that in winter it was bitterly cold. Sometimes when we woke up in the mornings, the water in our large container would be frozen solid. But the recompense was that we had a window, which meant that we could close the door (when we wanted to be alone) and still have light for reading and writing.

During our first winter we slept in the inner room. But it had a way of accumulating and retaining smoke from our own cooking fire and from Kalchu and Chola's next door. The following winter we decided that cold was preferable to smoke and we abandoned the inner room, using it only for storage. Even then it was a room we hated; it was pitch dark, day and night and, although we had a torch, it was almost always impossible to find whatever we were looking for. We called it the cave.

All three sections of the house – Kalchu's, his younger brother Māilo's and ours – led on to a shared flat roof. Above this roof and the living quarters was another flat roof and at the back of this there was a small shrine and a grain-storage room. In cross-section the house rose like a staircase. The various levels were connected by notched-pole ladders, and between the ground and the first floor there were two broader stone stairways.

When the family weren't eating, sleeping or out in the fields, they spent most of their time on the shared roof. This meant that, in effect, we had the best of both worlds: we were a self-contained unit and we were part of a larger extended family.

We paid Kalchu 60 rupees (about £2.50) rent per month. Later, when we realized we weren't going to be able to provide all the firewood we needed, we paid him 8 rupees for each load that he or one of his sons brought for us. We also bought most of our grain from him.

The usual method of field research in anthropology is called participant-observation. This means that the researcher spends as much time as possible being with people, doing whatever they happen to be doing, and learning by watching, listening and experiencing. In practice this is almost always combined with the use of interviews – partly because it's not always easy to tell where conversations that occur in the normal course of events shade into interviews, but also because it's often necessary to clarify and confirm the events you have witnessed.

Some anthropologists rely almost exclusively on interviews. This may be necessary if there is limited time; for example, if you can only go to a place in winter and need to research a summer festival, the best you can do is ask. But the main reason for substituting interviewing for participant-observation is convenience: you pay an informant whom you 'pump for information' in the comfort of your own home – and avoid 'getting your hands dirty'.

But interviewing as a research technique is notoriously problematical. As time went by, I began to see a pattern emerging of people answering my questions according to what I wanted to hear. Not only this, but I realized that they said they did things which, according to my later observations, they certainly did not. I began to understand how an over-reliance on interviews can systematically falsify your research. If you go to a place knowing next to nothing about the people, you can only base your questions on preconceptions, on a hypothesis you already have in mind. If the people you are interviewing then answer according to what you want to hear, the damage is already done. You have prejudged and pre-interpreted the very subject you are trying to investigate.

The idea of participant-observation – as opposed to interviewing – is that the anthropologist plays a passive role, allowing the people to define their lives themselves. Accordingly, in so far as this is possible, it undermines the anthropologist's preconceptions and conditioning. Participant-observation entailed, for us, a long and sometimes painful process of being humbled and then re-socialized. It was in this sense a soul journey.

During our first year in the village, most of our time was spent doing very basic things. Life was like a jigsaw puzzle that we were putting together slowly, piece by piece, with no idea what the end result would be.

People have often asked me what a typical day was like. We usually got up at dawn (partly because we were allowed no peace to sleep for longer) and went down to the stream to wash and fill our container with water. When we came back we lit a fire, kneaded the dough to make *rotis*, cooked and ate. Afterwards we sometimes joined the family working in the fields, sometimes washed clothes (a major undertaking), replastered the mud floor, which had to be done once a week, or visited other villages in the valley. Housework (including food preparation and cooking) took up a lot of time, and a lot of time was spent just being with people. In the evenings after we'd cooked and eaten, I tried to have some time to myself – learning vocabulary, recording the events of the day, reflecting.

This general routine took place in the context of the natural ebb and flow of village life. Sometimes, at weddings or festivals, we'd be very busy trying to see and do everything all at once. At other times, the days just rolled quietly by for months on end.

During the first year we went to Kathmandu twice to renew our visas. We went to Jumla about once every three weeks to collect our mail, to buy some more tea or kerosene for our lamp, to enjoy some English-speaking company or just for a change of scene.

When I think back over our time in Talphi, what stands out in my mind is our relationship with one family – Kalchu, Chola and their children – and their extraordinary kindness and generosity.

At first there was a certain amount of mutual mistrust between us. To a certain extent we tolerated each other for mercenary reasons – they got their money and the windfalls associated with foreigners, we got our information and photographs. But these attitudes were gradually replaced by bonds of genuine affection and concern.

The friendship inevitably deepened in proportion to our familiarity with the language. At first it was irritating and exhausting when people came into our room, sat down and talked non-stop without realizing or caring that we understood almost nothing – or alternatively, talked in words of one syllable that still made little sense. Later, talking became a pleasure, and eventually, the more we talked, the more we began to understand of village life, so were able to actually engage and empathize in conversations. Reaching the point where we could laugh and tease and be teased was like an initiation. After several months Kalchu taught us how to brew beer, which meant that between us we had a fairly regular supply – when his was finished ours had almost fermented and so on. Most evenings the three of us would sit together for a while, alone or with other villagers, drinking a bowl of beer and talking.

A large part of our relationship with the family and other people centred around their role as teachers, ours as pupils. This was true in the sense that they explained aspects of their lives to us as anthropologists; but they also taught us many of the basic skills of daily life. In their eyes we were like babies; we knew almost nothing, except how to read and write – which for their purposes were irrelevant anyway.

It was Kāli, a child of about ten, who taught me most of the simple skills that every village woman knows; how to husk rice, how to grind grain in the water-mill, how to make the different kinds of *roṭis*, how to dress in local clothes, how to replaster the floor of the house. She even taught me what to do when I was menstruating: that I shouldn't fetch water, cook, or touch any man.

This was part of the process by which we were humbled and then re-socialized. And although everyone in the family, even the children, were patient, sympathetic teachers, it was sometimes hard for us to feel both so useless and so indebted. Maybe this was one reason why, when people came to us for medicine, as they did from the very beginning, it would have been impossible not to attempt to treat them. We tried to explain that we weren't doctors and had almost no medicine, but no one believed us. So we used up our own medical supplies, then brought some more from Kathmandu and resigned ourselves to the role of paramedics. Often we felt almost paralysed by our incompetence in the face of some of the terrible diseases and afflictions we were trusted to cure. But it was the one thing that people asked of us: the one thing we could usefully do.

There were many times when the whole concept of anthropological field-work seemed impossibly difficult. For our part, we never really came to terms with some of the physical discomforts that were part of everyone else's accepted reality. The smoke from the fire was a constant source of irritation; the houses were designed with the fire in the centre of the room. There were no chimneys and the only way for the smoke to escape was through a narrow gap between the wall and the eaves. Everyone split their firewood so it burned more easily; we chopped ours particularly finely, but still our eyes and noses streamed continually. In the end Kalchu let us cut a hole in the roof to serve as a chimney; we sacrificed a chicken first to stop the hole being used for access to the house by evil spirits. But the chimney only worked on windless days. At other times the smoke would still be blown hither and thither and we continued to suffer from headaches and coughs along with everyone else.

The other thing I hated was being so dirty. The smoke from the pitch-pine burned for lighting soon turned all our possessions black: clothes, books, sleeping-bags. In no time at all our hands and faces were permanently ingrained with soot. In winter the river-water was numbingly cold, so we heated our water and washed in a bowl by the fireside – quietly, because we were contravening the rules of household purity. Several times – when I had lice, fleas, worms and diarrhoea all at once – I actually dreamt of a bathroom.

For the villagers, having anthropologists in their midst gave rise to feelings of envy. People continually pointed out how easy our lot was compared to theirs: we were fat and healthy; we had good food to eat; we had medicine, contraception, money; we didn't have to work in the fields and could sit at home all day reading and writing.

It also made them suspicious. People (with the possible exception of the family we lived with) never really knew what we were doing there. Sometimes rumours would start that we were going to evacuate several of the local villages and set up a hunting reserve for foreigners, and people would come up to us asking when we were going to send them away. At other times, when we were taking a photograph or writing down what someone had said, they'd look at us intently and ask what all this information was *really* for.

Inevitably this upset us. One day the whole situation seemed so intolerable that I almost resolved to leave. It was during our first monsoon. The room was thick with flies – I've never seen flies like those before or since – and I was washing dishes. People had been pouring into our room all day, staring at us, pointing and commenting as though we were animals in a zoo, and I'd been rude and bad-tempered to them all. As I was scrubbing the soot-blackened pans with ash and charcoal, I remember looking down at my filthy hands in the bowl of greasy water with bits of charcoal floating on the surface, and realizing in a flash that I could just get up and go – and how very happy that would make me.

But I didn't go – because there was another side to it: I was infatuated with the village. I loved the slow simplicity of the subsistence farmer's life: how going to work meant growing food to eat; how everything was acted out against a backdrop of the landscape, the weather and the seasons. For all its hardships, life had a basic logic that we've long since lost in the West. I loved the absence of shops and advertising, the purity of children who'd never watched television, the great pleasure of eating different foods as they ripened with the seasons – the first wild greens and strawberries, a rare bowl of milk in summer – as opposed to our own processed and preserved permanent supplies. But most of all I loved the occasional feeling that we belonged, like the time I became *mitini* (ritual friend) with Jakali; and like the time we came back from Kathmandu with fishing hooks and lines, spices and photographs as presents, and were invited to house after house for celebratory meals.

When we'd been in the village a year, I began to read through my field notes and assess the state of my research. It worried me slightly that my knowledge of the village was so impressionistic –

gained entirely from participant-observation and conversations, mainly with Kalchu – and lacking in what you might call 'facts'. I remembered what other anthropologists had told me: if all else fails, approach the school teacher. There wasn't one in Talphi at that time, so I went to Māthichaur, a village several miles away, where the small school catered for all the children of neighbouring villages whose parents could spare them from work in the fields.

The four teachers, Ṭasi, Nara Bahādur, Chandan (from neighbouring villages) and Keśāb (from Jumla Bazaar), were sympathetic to my problem and suggested that I come over sometimes in the afternoon, when school was over, with my pen and notebook. These sessions turned out to be invaluable. On the days before I went I prepared various subjects – for example, caste, religion, kinship or education – reviewing all the information I had gathered myself, rereading the few existing accounts of the same subject in comparable areas, and vaguely preparing questions.

The biggest advantage of working with the teachers (apart from the fact that they weren't always out in the fields) was quite simply that they were educated. Unlike the majority of villagers, they were able to conceptualize and think in abstract terms, which is necessary to dissect a subject and dwell on details. When I tried to get Kalchu to discuss an idea out of context, he very quickly lost interest – it wasn't his way of talking.

In fact, even the teachers found it difficult. It was an advantage that Keśāb, like me, was an outsider, so the two of us were able to join forces in coaxing the others to distance themselves from things they'd always taken for granted, in order to objectify and explain them. But the real blessing was that Keśāb was the only person I knew (apart from Peter) who could speak some English.

I came to really look forward to those afternoons in Māthichaur – we all did, I think. About once a week, all through that winter, we'd sit around the fire in the small schoolroom, roasting potatoes in the embers, drinking Tibetan tea (Māthichaur was the only village of Tibetans in the area), talking and laughing.

But towards spring the sessions gradually became less regular.

Often I'd walk over to Māthichaur at the appointed time, only to be told that there'd been no school that day because the teachers had been busy with the ploughing or the sowing, or they'd had to go to Jumla to pick up their wages. Eventually the sessions petered out completely, although each of the teachers would sometimes drop in to see us. Keśāb remained a firm friend – helping us in every possible way – for the rest of the time we were there.

When the time was coming for us to leave the village, someone would invite us to their house to eat almost every day, and we were given gifts – a small purse knitted by Sigarup, a necklace of different-coloured tiny beads woven by Kāli, a plaited red-and-white woollen belt.

On the day we left, I replastered the floor of our house – to Hindus, foreigners are, strictly speaking, untouchable, partly because we have a history of eating beef. In Talphi this attitude had scarcely been intimated, yet to me it was important that we didn't leave their home in any way polluted.

We ate our last meal with Kalchu and Chola – *puris* and rice with curd, and some beer which Kalchu had brewed specially. People we had known came in to wish us well and brought us parcels of food for the journey – rounds of buckwheat bread and roasted amaranthus seeds in honey, wrapped in birch-bark.

Later, all those people stood on the roof and watched us getting ready to go. We were still wearing our local clothes, but as we put on our rucksacks I knew that we were once again looking like foreigners and tourists. Kalchu and Chola marked yellow *ṭikās* on our foreheads and we returned them. There's no word in the local dialect for 'thank-you', so we used the Kathmandu '*dhanyabād*' to thank them again for their hospitality. There were any number of other things I urgently wanted to tell them, but suddenly all my Nepāli had gone. So when they said, 'Go well', we simply replied, 'Stay well'.

When we were outside the village, I suddenly realized that Kāli hadn't been at home as we were leaving. In my confusion I hadn't noticed. I was about to go back and say goodbye when I saw her on the path ahead, grazing the cattle. She looked very shy as we approached and didn't want to catch my eye. I felt an over-whelming desire to hug her, but I didn't. I just told her that I'd left my sari that she'd so much wanted with her mother – and she smiled at that.

In the years since we left Talphi, Peter has been back three times. He tells me that Kalchu and Chola and the children have been pleased to see him and are as warm and generous as they ever were. He also tells me the news of the village; who has been married, who has had a child, whose son now has a government job in Jumla. I haven't been back. For the time being, the memory is as much as my senses can process.

PART I

LEARNING TO UNDERSTAND
A CATTLE OWNER

I once asked Kalchu how he was able to tell his cows one from the other, and how he was able to distinguish his own from other people's. To me all the cows looked similar – small and black all over although I did recognize that some had longer horns and a few had none at all. He looked at me and said he often wondered how I told my books apart. To him they looked the same.

We smiled, acknowledging the difference of our worlds.

THE CALF WAS BORN A MONTH PREMATURELY, IN MARCH. THE nights were still so cold that icicles formed on the outside of the chutes that fed the water-mills, where the water churned white and spilled over. In the day they dripped steadily and almost thawed, and then from dusk to the following sunrise they were slowly reformed. As far as the eye could see the earth was brown; there were white pockets of unmelted snow, and sombre green pine thickets on the ridges, but no leaves on the deciduous trees and no bright green shoots in the withered remains of last year's grass. Nothing was ready for new life.

I don't know what alerted Kalchu to go and look in the stable. He may have heard the cow moaning as she gave birth, his ears sensitized to noises the rest of us would not have heard, as we sat talking and laughing around the fire. Or maybe he had seen the onset of labour in the way she had acted earlier, when he and Kāli untwisted the bales of hay for the night and spread out the fresh pine-needle bedding. He was gone for about half an hour and I don't think any of us even suspected that there was something amiss.

When he came back he was carrying the calf, his arms encompassing all four legs, so the hooves came together in a bunch, with the rump and tail protruding over one forearm and the shoulders and chest over the other. The neck was stretched out in front so the head hung down low, almost as low as the tiny hooves.

Inside he twisted round and, leaning his shoulder and elbow against the door, pushed it firmly to. Then, very gently, he lowered the calf on to the rug by the fireside. As soon as the hooves touched the ground the legs crumpled and carefully he rearranged them, folding them over to one side, out of the way of the body. Comfortable now, and secure in the warmth, the calf let its neck curl round – an almost involuntary movement – so the chin skirted the ribs and the muzzle nudged the soft hollow flank. Its ears rested flat back and the long dark lashes interlocked over closed eyes. It could almost have been dead already; a passive progression from birth to death with no awareness of life at all.

The twins sprang up from where they had been sitting by Chola's side and ran round the hearth to have a closer look. Squatting down naked by the calf they stroked it and ran their small fingers through its coat. There were no traces of blood now, just a damp oily film where the mother's tongue had licked it clean. Lāla Bahādur started to play with its stringy tail – twirling it round in the air, twisting and tugging it back from the socket – trying to provoke a reaction that would jar it to life. But Hārkini just touched it gently all over, marvelling at the tiny, perfect form.

At first no one was quite sure what should be done. Kalchu sat silently watching the calf. He seemed resigned to this twist of fate that the first calf to be born into his stable for two years had been brought to life before it was ready, before the winter was even through. There was no emotion in his face – no resentment, no sadness. If there had been its time had passed. Now he merely appraised the situation, calculating the odds for life against death. In the end he judged that the investment of hope should be made; that they would fight for the calf's life and risk disappointment.

His decision resolved the confused inactivity. If the calf was to be kept alive the course of action was clear and time was critical. Nara was sent to get a bowl of milk from someone who had a cow that was yielding; Kalchu suggested maybe the *ḍāṅgri* or the *Ḍum* in the bottom house on the corner. At this time of year there wasn't enough milk anywhere in the village to borrow for more than a few days. So if the mother was still dry then, there would be no choice but to let the calf starve.

'I suppose I could always suckle it myself – give the twins one breast and the calf the other.' Chola was leaning back laughing, making as if to enfold the old and new progeny under her two arms. 'It's been done before – twice when calves were born to dry mothers, the women of the household fed them their own breast-milk until they were old enough to wean.' I looked at her dubiously, and she was still laughing and insisting that it was true. But it was impossible to distinguish between the truth of myth and the truth of reality.

While we were discussing it, Kalchu was trying to inspire the calf with life. He opened its eyes, and standing astride the small body, he clasped it between his rough hands and pulled it up. When the hooves were in place on the ground he held the weight for a moment while the calf reoriented itself. Then he let go. Clearly there was some innate sense of balance: the calf lowered its head and stretched out its neck, then reeled slightly and righted itself. But the muscles had no strength to sustain it, and it fell over forwards, hitting its nose on the ground.

When Kalchu pulled it up again there was blood trickling from its nostril. This time it held out longer, and gradually it learned the way to work its muscles and to develop their strength. Eventually it was standing so well that the twins were able to play teasing games with it, pushing and pulling and slapping its sides, so sometimes it fell and sometimes it lurched from side to side and recovered. And we cheered and laughed at its chequered progress – and picked it up again and again because it was still too weak to get up alone.

The will and ability to stand is one of the most basic manifestations of the life-force, almost more basic than an interest in food and water. I'd seen this attitude once before in the village when a cow, grazing on the cliffside, fell down into the valley below. There was no doubt that its foreleg was broken; it was bent right out to the side from the knee. But it was a valuable animal with many calves to its name and the owners hovered over it, beating it viciously, insisting that it stand up. Eventually it did. You could see that the pain of standing was more than it could bear, and it struggled to be allowed to collapse again but the owners made it walk; led it away stumbling on three legs with the fourth jutting out sideways. And they were triumphant, as we were now, because it was a sign that it was going to be all right: a clear confirmation of life.

When Nara came back with the milk, the calf had collapsed, exhausted. Its legs were splayed out at awkward angles on the rug, and its flanks rose and fell with the deep breaths of sleep. He had found milk at the *ḍāṅgri's* house and the old man had come back with him to see if he could be of any use. He didn't advise but just stood there, nodding his head vaguely and smiling to himself while his hands – almost involuntarily – went through the motions of twisting the spindle he'd brought with him and winding on the wool. Then he sat down quietly, reluctant to flaunt the experience of his years unsolicited.

And there was no doubt that Kalchu, though younger, had dealt with a great many premature births before this one. He handled the calf deftly, with calm assurance. None of us did anything; we sat there silently watching, deferring to his competence. He was pulling back the calf's head so the brown eyes rolled up and only the whites were showing, and opening its mouth by slipping his thumb in at the side. Then, keeping the thumb in place, he pushed the rim of a bowl in between the rows of teeth and poured its contents, a trickle of oil, right down into the throat. The calf shook its head lamely, but Kalchu merely tightened his hold and stroked the underneath of the throat to make it swallow. Then he let go and the calf sank back to sleep. 'That's to make him shit,' he said. I wondered why it was important that it shat, but I didn't ask. Maybe it was no more than another way of affirming its life.

The next thing was to make it eat and drink. So, lifting up its head again, Kalchu offered it a finger coated with milk. It was very weary now, so weary it only wanted to drop back to sleep, and yet too weary to fight for that freedom. It ignored the finger and Kalchu dipped it into the milk again and forcibly opened the mouth. 'If they don't suck by the second day,' said the *ḍāṅgri*, 'they forget how.' So Kalchu persevered, and the calf reached out its tongue and licked his finger, and then, at last, took it inside its mouth and sucked.

Before we went to bed we took the calf down to the stable to its mother. 'It's important that they see each other tonight,' Kalchu explained. 'If the mother thinks her calf is dead, she'll dry up for good. And the little one will lose heart and its life will drift away if it's cut off for too long from its own animal world.'

It was pitch dark in the stable and, even with the burning sticks of *jharo* we'd brought from upstairs, we could see nothing at first. But it felt safe and familiar as it always did, with the sounds of chewing and the smell of sweat and cow-dung and half-eaten hay. In the end the mother found us, grunting softly as she came over, nuzzling the calf and licking its cheek and neck.

When they had reassured each other, Kalchu put the calf down by her side. She still hadn't completely shed the afterbirth and it was hanging down, a twisted sheet of blood and mucus, between her legs. As he pushed the calf's head towards the udder he spat to rid himself of the polluting sight of birth.

The calf didn't recognize the teat, but standing there by its mother's side it shat. And Kalchu was satisfied and picked up the quivering body to carry it back to the fireside.

The next morning each of us went in turn, as we woke, to have a look at the calf. It was more alert today, staring out at its surroundings through moist brown eyes that were learning to focus, and playing with swishing its tail. But it seemed very small, much smaller and more fragile than the night before, as it swayed from side to side in the bright sunlight. And I noticed that the skin was hanging loose in folds over the shoulder and behind it, as if it had fit a rounder form yesterday, before the rigours of birth. 'The mother's still dry.' Kalchu had anticipated my question. 'We'll have to see it through a few more days ourselves.'

It was a job that fell mainly to me, because I was at home. Kalchu and Chola were both out all day at that time, preparing the winter land for spring. In the mornings they left the calf outside on the roof, under an upturned basket to stop the crows and vultures swooping down to peck out its eyes, and because sometimes, in winter, the jackals are driven by hunger right up to the houses, even in daylight. Then they draped a rug over the basket, so the calf could be warmed by the sun, but not dazzled by its rays. I found a medicine dropper and used that to feed it the milk they left me. And when I went out I put the calf inside with its basket and rug.

In the evenings, when Kāli brought the cows home, we'd take it down to the stable to its mother and she would stretch out her nose to it and blow, and the breath would come out as steam in the cold, evening air. But she had no milk to give it – so there was no reason for it to suck the teat, which would have helped the flow.

After ten days the calf had become a haunting presence. Its body was hot and dry and the coat had lost its black lustre, so it stood up on end, pale brown and rumpled. Most of the time it looked dead. Its breathing was too light to move the flanks, so I'd go over sometimes and put the back of my hand to its nostril until I could feel the heat as it exhaled. Its eyes were no longer the eyes of a cow – they were blue and vacant, like the eyes of a mad person sending images to the brain of a world other than it really is. It rarely blinked, but sometimes the lids would close and then reopen, as if consciousness were slowly drifting away.

One night I dreamt about it; about the dog going over to look at it, as it sometimes did, and instead of sniffing it and walking away, it tore open the anus and started to pull out the innards.

I still fed it, but I recoiled from it. I hated pushing the medicine dropper in between the rows of teeth, now permanently bared, and the hot dry lips, and watching the milk dribble out at the corner because it wouldn't swallow. Kalchu and Chola had lost interest in it, like animals with their dying young. Sometimes they'd stand it up and watch it fall over, as if justifying their negligence. Then they let it be.

One morning Kalchu came up from the stable with a bowl of warm milk and poured half of it into a separate container for me.

He was pleased, proud that his was one of the few households with milk in winter, and apparently unruffled by the irony of its coming too late, when the calf was already more dead than alive.

The calf lived for fifteen days. It was sad when it died; sad because of the memory of what it had been like when there was still hope. But it was also a relief. I didn't see it dead. The Ḍum leatherworker came and took away the body very early one morning. Then, some days later, he brought it back – stuffed. The fur was very dull now, and sparse, and the eyes were gaping black holes in their sockets. It was a rough job, but somehow it didn't look that different with the skin stretched over straw instead of ribs. Kalchu took it downstairs to the stable twice a day when he milked the mother. He said that the dummy stimulated her to produce in the same way that the sight of the living calf should have done.

Then, not a week later, one of the ploughing bulls seemed to be ailing. Kalchu had been working them, tilling the land on the south-facing slope of Jimale, where wheat and bitter buckwheat are sown alternately. Those upland fields are the hardest land of all to till, not only because of the incline, but also because they've recently been reclaimed from the forest and the soil is still heavy with roots and stones. He had been careful not to push the bulls too hard. In the evening when they came back he would crumble salt on a flat stone for them to lick, and once, in addition to their hay, he gave them the heap of grain that was left at the bottom of the fermentation jar when the beer was finished. Usually, he said, after ploughing for four or five days, he would keep the bulls at home for two. But this time only one had rested; the other had worked right through, for a full ten days. This was because Jakali's husband's ploughing bull had died and he'd pleaded with Kalchu to lend him one of his.

So now it was ill. There were no visible symptoms. Kalchu had gone right round it, feeling its legs and back and stomach, but he could find nothing. There were no cuts or swollen bruises, nowhere that was particularly tender or sensitive to his touch. He assumed that it was exhausted, wasted by the work at the end of the long winter, and he blamed himself. He had lent it to Jakali's husband against his better judgement. He had felt sorry for him when his own bull died and he was afraid it would be tempting fate to throw up this opportunity to redress the balance in their fortunes. And if it was just exhausted, it was simply a question of postponing his own ploughing and resting it up for a day or two until it had regained its appetite and its strength.

But a week passed, and then ten days, and there was no change at all. It just stood there, or sometimes lay down, in one particular spot at the far end of the stable, with its eyes half-closed. There was none of the violence of illness in it, no writhing or moaning, and it was never impatient or irritable when Kalchu tried to feed it or probed it for sores. Nor was there any instinctive offensive, no fight to transcend its condition and stay alive. It was as if it was harbouring some great consuming sadness and had lost the urge to live.

One morning a *Dumini* from Pere came to have a look at it. She was a *mantri*, a person who knew certain magic incantations, and was reputed to be able to cure sick animals. She told Chola she'd heard from someone in Pere that the bull was ill, and she knew she'd be able to cure it; she'd treated hundreds in her time and only one had ever died.

So Chola took her downstairs and led the bull out of its dark stable into the adjoining sheep-pen, which was enclosed by stone walls, but without a roof so there was light to see. The *mantri* looked it up and down from the doorway without saying a word. Then she sent Nara to fetch the things she would need: a piece of rope the length of the space between her hands when she held out her arms; a supple willow twig, the length of the space between Nara's hands; a sprig of the *dāntelo* bush in flower; and some wheat flour and tobacco for her own payment.

Then, still in silence, she picked up some cow-dung from the floor and rolled it into a ball between her fingertips. When it was the right shape she blew on it, then closed her fist around it and began to massage the bull's neck and shoulders and back and rump, tapping it hard and rhythmically with the knuckles of the clenched fist. All the time she was muttering under her breath, not articulating the words so they could be understood, or so it was even clear what language she was speaking. But her lips were moving fast and her voice rose and fell between breaths. It seemed that all her concentration and all the power of every muscle in her body were focused on the point where her fist struck the bull's back.

And strangely, the bull was responding, shifting its weight from one side to the other, so it was leaning slightly towards her. And around each blow the flesh shuddered – the same sort of involuntary movement a cow will use to despatch a fly, but the ripples were more pronounced and further-reaching.

While the *mantri* was working, Chola stood in front of the bull, holding its head down low and gently smoothing the tuft of coarse hair between the horns, reassuring it.

It took the *mantri* a long time to work right round the bull, from shoulder to rump down one side and then from rump to shoulder back up the other. When she had finished she turned to Nara, who had just come back with the things she needed and was peering round the door, as if he was too scared of her magic to come right in. 'Take this to the crossroads,' she said, dropping the ball of cow-dung into his cupped hands, 'and bury it so none of it's left showing.'

Then she took the willow twig, laid it across the bull's withers and secured it in place with a rope tied firmly beneath the soft folds of flesh on the underside of the neck. 'That represents its ploughing yoke,' she told Chola. 'Leave it there. In due course he'll rub it off himself.'

On her way out she paused, reaching up to slot the *dāṅtelo* branch between the stones above the lintel, and the bull lowered its head threateningly and took a few steps towards her as if it was going to lunge. But then it turned round towards the open stable door and went back to its place in the darkness,

Chola had taken the bull's high spirits and responsiveness to the *mantri* as a sign that the treatment was going to work. But in the following days nothing changed. When Kalchu brought it fresh hay and water and even maize porridge it remained aloof and indifferent. And when the other cows were taken out in the morning and brought home in the evening, it stood there without even turning its head. And the days passed and the nights passed and it seemed to be just waiting for death.

The next time the *dhāmi* was possessed by one of the village gods, Kalchu went to the shrine to ask for advice. And the god, speaking in his high falsetto voice through the medium of the *dhāmi*, said without a moment's hesitation that Kalchu's bull's time had come, and there was nothing any of us could do to save it now. He added that two of Kalchu's bulls would die this winter and the third would live. After that the bull's willow twig yoke was replaced by a strip of red cloth blessed by the god. It was fastened tightly on to the right horn, so it dangled down over the cheek and eye.

The *dhāmi* was right. Nothing could restore the bull's heart for life. One evening Kalchu came into my room and we sat staring into the fire for a long time. Then he said that the bull had died. He had gone down to the stable earlier and seen that it was missing, so he went to look for it. He couldn't believe that it would have wandered far when it hadn't even been outside the stable for such a long time.

He searched everywhere for it, going right through the village, asking people if they'd seen it. But no one knew. Eventually, he found it, lying down on the Kālādika – an open, grassy plateau about a quarter of a mile outside the village – the nearest place where the cattle were taken to graze. There was a young boy there with his cows at the time, and he told Kalchu that he had watched the bull and it had walked slowly right round the circumference of the Kālādika, before lying down where Kalchu had found it. It wasn't dead, but it was dying.

'I took a bowl of water and I gave it *hirin*, as if it was my father, or my brother,' said Kalchu. 'And then it died and I came home.'

I was shocked. I hadn't realized the bull meant so much to him.

'It ploughed my land for eight years. It knew better than I did what to do. It even knew which land was mine so I needn't even have guided it there. It was part of my family. It was part of me.'

I thought back over the times I had watched the ploughing; in late autumn at the potato harvest, and in the summer, slopping through the flooded paddy fields. There had never seemed to be a particularly harmonious relationship between Kalchu and the bulls. They had minds of their own, refusing to move one minute, and the next tearing ahead out of control, breaking down the mud banks that contained the irrigation between the paddy fields. And Kalchu would alternately soothe and cajole and then whip and curse them. There was no doubt he spoke a language the bulls understood, but no one could say they always obeyed him.

'But you have other bulls, don't you?' I asked.

'Yes,' he said sadly. 'Two. But they're young. They're not strong enough and they haven't been trained.' He sat silently for a minute and then he got up and walked out.

And still that wasn't the end of it. Not long afterwards one of the cows died. It happened at night in the stable, and in the morning the Untouchable women came and dragged it outside and butchered it just in front of the house. Kalchu and Chola were both at home and from time to time they looked down, both repelled and fascinated. And villagers walking past gave the gathering a wide berth, and spat in disgust with disparaging comments. But the women were crouched so low over their work that their shawls shrouded their whole bodies, and I didn't once see them raise their eyes from the carcass. It took them most of the day and, in the evening, they picked up their basketloads of red meat and carried them back to the security and acceptance of their own Untouchable community at the far end of the village.

But it wasn't just Kalchu and Chola's cows that were dying, and it wasn't just bad luck either. They said that every year at the end of winter the cows are so thin and weak that diseases spread and wipe them out like flies. And if the spring is late, like this year, then the supplies of hay that the women gathered all autumn from the steepest slopes where the grass grew longer because it couldn't be grazed just don't last out. Everyone's cows suffer.

Last year too the spring was late and Jakali and her husband lost so many cows that they consulted the god. The god said that the place where their house and stable were built was plagued with evil influences. So they took the house apart, stone by stone, and rebuilt it twenty yards further south on a piece of land recommended by the god. They built it around a makeshift shrine, with offerings to the gods, both good and bad, and it took them all the following winter, this winter. And it was then, when Jakali's husband's ploughing bull died despite the new stable, that Kalchu had felt obliged to lend him his, and it had been over-worked and died.

THE FULL-MOON FESTIVAL AND THE STORY OF THE *MAṢṬĀ* GODS

On certain occasions when the dhāmi *is possessed, the god he embodies tells the story of his life. These stories are known as* paṛelis.

In essence all paṛelis *are similar; they tell of how the* Maṣṭā Gods *(the Bāra Bhāi or Twelve Brothers) wander the earth until they come to a place that they like in particular. Here they make the land habitable, banish evil spirits (or convert them into lesser deities, the Bāhan) and care for the people.*

The paṛeli *that follows is composite, made up of extracts from many different* paṛelis. *Most of these were recorded by Gabriel Campbell and Tunga Nath Upadaya in various villages in the Jumla area. The transcription and initial translation into English were done by Gabriel Campbell, Prithivi Raj Chettri and Tunga Nath Upadaya.*

> With the permission and orders of the
> king of heaven, Indra, I have crossed
> mountains and rivers and hills and
> other strange and lonely places and
> have come to this world of the mortals.

IT'S THE TIME OF THE *karāti*, THE NIGHTS LEADING UP TO THE full-moon festival, when the gods enter the *dhāmis* and use their bodies to dance among the villagers. Somewhere people are drumming – it must be at the far end of the village, because at times the rhythm is distinct but when the wind takes it it becomes muffled, merging with the roar of the full monsoon river.

Later, well into the night, Mina and Kāli wrap blankets round their shoulders and walk out through the village. Dogs mark their progress, a different one barking from each rooftop they pass. They sound anxious tonight and fierce, troubled by the full moon and the drums. When they reach the source of the drumming they climb up one ladder and then another on to the top roof of the house.

Already there's a crowd – men, women, boys and girls, toddlers and babies. The door of the shrine at the back of the roof is open. Inside there's a group of men sitting round the fire, their faces striped with flames and shadows. Outside young girls in pairs hold hands facing each other and, leaning back, they pirouette so fast that their shawls flare out from the tops of their heads. One young boy streaks through the darkness, like a small fish, in and out of the groups, stinging ankles with a handful of cut nettles, then melting into the shadows before the inevitable angry rebukes.

> I have plucked flowers from twenty-two
> pastures and twenty-two mountains and

> from plateaux and green lowland meadows.
> There are flowers of nine different
> colours, and I gathered them and put
> them into my hair out of sheer joy, and
> they have become part of me.

The drum-beat intensifies. The musicians are sitting in a row on the edge of the roof, facing inwards. Their drums, half spheres of hand-worked copper, are laid out in a line in front of them. They're pounding them with bent drumsticks, hard and fast, with all the strength of their hands and wrists. The roof is vibrating. Inside the shrine the bells start ringing, rhythmically clanging as they swing up and down, round in an arc as the cord is pulled and released. Close by the doorway two boys clash cymbals, hard so they hit together squarely, hollow full against cupped hollow. Next to them a baby shrieks in its mother's arms.

> For twelve years I have wandered through
> different places. I have walked in the
> truth and spoken in strength. I have
> shaken twenty-two regions with my power.
> And I have done much that is good as
> well. I have made places of pilgrimage,
> and cared for their pilgrims. I have
> built temples. On the banks of a lake,
> in a place called Garagāli, there was a
> temple inlaid with gold and silver, and
> when you saw that temple, even if you
> had never wept in your life, tears would
> fill your eyes and you would weep.

A man sitting in a group, leaning against the wall of the shrine, starts shaking and stands up, throwing aside the woollen blanket he wears as a shawl and kicking off his shoes. His body still convulsing, he fumbles to untie his turban and release the long twisted tuft of hair, the *dhāmi*'s insignia, that's always covered from sight except when he's possessed – when he becomes the god. The crowd clears back and he moves into the middle of the roof.

Standing alone in this pool of moonlight, he puts his thumb and forefinger into the corners of his mouth and, staring out across the houses and the fields and the river valley to the stark moonlit mountains, whistles long and loud into the night.

For an instant the moon disappears. The sky is still bright and the roof illuminated, but where the moon had been there are now heavy black storm-clouds brightly outlined in white light. Then it slides back, perfect in its pale roundness.

The *dhāmi* stands motionless before it. It seems for a moment as if the world is peopled only by this god and this moon, facing each other through the aeons of the night. His face is unearthly – eyes glazed in concentration, cheekbones and jaw protruding floodlit from heavy black shadows.

He disappears for a minute into the shrine and returns with two pairs of bells and with a yellow *ṭīkā* marked between his eyes. He begins to dance, holding the bells – a pair in each hand – rigid by his groin. He dances to the rhythm of the bells and the drums and the cymbals, moving fast, careening about from one end of the roof to the other. His arms hardly move at all – just the legs move, and his bare feet on the ground as he jumps up and down, and the long tuft of hair that bounces back and forth over his shoulder. He's wearing white, the only white on the roof, a symbol of his purity. He wears white for the same reason that he never drinks *raksi*, and that he's eaten no food since morning. It's a mark of reverence that the vehicle provided for the god to come to his people is pure and empty and won't pollute.

> One place especially was beautiful.
> The mist would blow off the top of the
> mountains and there were always a few
> fine clouds and a light rain. It gave
> me so much pleasure. And near that
> plateau was a forest of larch and
> evergreen oak. And below it the wide-

open grassland. There I took twenty-two
stakes and in twenty-two hours I
pegged them into the ground and marked
out twenty-two boundaries.

Another *dhāmi* has joined him and they link arms for a while
and then move closer together, stretching their arms across each
other's shoulders so they dance as one, their bodies tilting first
forwards and then back as they bounce across the roof. They're
brothers, two of the Bāra Bhāi, the twelve *Maṣṭā* gods. They're
smiling, eyes ablaze, lost in each other's presence, in the dance.

They embrace, then separate, and one goes over to a woman
in the crowd with a child cradled in her arms. She talks to him,
anxiously tilting her face upwards so it's exposed and openly
imploring, a look designed to tap compassion. He answers without
looking at her, his eyes focused on space, on the moonlight. His
voice is high-pitched and breathless, floating in the back of the
mouth, instead of pushing up from the throat and chest. It's a
voice that doesn't belong to one of the villagers and she seems
not to understand; maybe she can't even hear, above the bellow
of the drums.

Still twitching and shuddering, as if to the beat of the wrong
pulse, the *dhāmi* locks at the child, willing his eyes to focus, be still.
Standing close above it, he presses the rim of a bell hard against
its skull and, leaning forward, blows a blast of air into each ear,
one after the other. Then he stands back and, from a distance,
sprays the child's face with a fistful of rice grains, and dances away.

There are three of them dancing now, sometimes together,
sometimes separately, all in white. Without warning one falls out
of step and drops back to his place in the crowd. Panting and
breathless, but no longer shaking, he takes hold of his tuft of hair,
winds it into a coil on top of his head and reties his turban. His
god has left him.

The other *dhāmis* carry on dancing for a while and then their
gods go too. The bells in the shrine have stopped ringing and

gradually the drumming abates and the vibrations are stilled.

People spill back across the empty space of moonlight, and the dancers' faces merge with the crowd. Someone is closing the double doors of the shrine, fastening the chain latch, and firelight flickers out dimly between the slats.

> There were rocks and boulders that made
> it difficult to walk to and from that
> place. Those rocks and boulders were
> like mountains. And I took my stick
> and swung it round, and my power was so
> great and so terrible that the hills
> and mountains shook. And I split that
> place in two and made a path for people
> to come and go, and for their sheep and
> goats.
> And there was little water in that place.
> So when I saw that, I dug my knee into
> the ground and water welled up beneath
> and flowed out around it. And I dug
> wells of milk and wells of oil. And I
> sowed seeds and grew plants and trees so
> that that place would be still more
> beautiful.

Ekādaśi, duadaśi, tetradaśi, chaturdaśi: the days of the *karāti*, when the gods dance at night. Then follows the day of the full moon, *purnimā*, and the full-moon festival, called the *paiṭh*. It dawns sunny and clear, with a strong wind blowing, and storms of chaff from the barley-threshing on the roof rain down yellow against a peacock sky.

No work is done in the fields today and Kalchu is sitting in the sun, making a necklace of marigolds by sinking a needle into the yellow hearts and sliding them together along coarse black thread. Chola is replastering the floor with fresh mud and cow-dung in deference to the gods' visit. Since early morning there has been intermittent drumming in different parts of the village and the echo rolls round the valley like the stifled rumblings of a caged lion.

> There was a demon called Bānba, and
> he was king of all the demons. There
> was a great battle between Bānba and
> myself. We fought for seven days and
> seven nights. Then I chained him to
> the four corners of the earth, and I
> danced on his chest and sat on his
> back. There was blood streaming from
> his mouth and nose, and he was
> frightened and said that he would
> leave that place and would go to the
> underworld. I made him take an oath
> that he would never frighten anyone or
> cause them any harm – only then did I
> let him go. He even licked my feet –
> first he wanted to fight, then he
> licked my feet. That made me laugh.

Mina and Kāli are taking their offering for the festival to the house where the *dhāmis* have been dancing at night. Mina is carrying the wheat flour in a bronze plate and the oil in a smaller bronze bowl bedded inside it. They pass a group of boys, a jangling procession, on their way to wash the temple bells in the stream – their annual cleansing and consecration. They wait in turn while the *ḍāṅgri*, dressed in white, measures other households' offerings.

Two *mānās* of flour is the quota, plus one ladle of oil that's poured into a wide-mouthed container so that the yellow mustard oil, the greener walnut and hemp-seed oils and the cloudy melted ghee combine.

Later in the afternoon, while most people are still washing and dressing and getting ready, the preparations begin at the shrine high above the village, on a plateau under the shade of two juniper trees. The wind is even stronger at this height. It carries

44

the scent of pine and tosses the juniper branches back and forth across the sun, so the ground and the roof of the shrine are slashed with creeping shadows.

The *ḍāṅgri* is there, plastering the floor with a wash of red mud and cow-dung, filling and lighting the oil lamps, burning some sprigs of juniper as incense. That's in the darkness of the inner room, with its raised seat for the *dhāmi* when he's possessed, and its rows of bells and strips of red and white cotton cloth strung in a jumble from the rafters.

Outside on the veranda, where the eaves are supported by pillars crowned with carved wooden rams' heads and the real skulls and horns of sacrificed rams and he-goats, two men are kneading the dough for *puris*, pummelling the flour of every household in the village. They're talking and laughing as they work. Beside them, tethered to the corner post, are six lambs. One is alert and quietly bleating; the others are lying crumpled in a heap of fluffy whiteness in the sunshine.

It's almost evening when Kalchu climbs up the hill carrying Hārkini on his back with Kāli, Nara and Lāla Bahādur following behind. The shrine is packed with people. Children cram themselves into the doorway and cling to the window, like moths to light, hoping to catch a glimpse of the possessed *dhāmi*. Inside, the god is reciting his *paṛeli*, the story of his wanderings through the earth before he settled in the village. And people are asking for advice and blessings, telling him about the problems they trust him to solve.

Outside the shrine the crowd is waiting. Almost everyone is there – the whole village dressed in its festival finery. The musicians, six or seven of them, are crouched in a row behind their drums, playing abstractedly until the dancing begins. One of the juniper trees is enlaced with the spread-eagled bodies of children, fighting for the highest branches and the best view of the dancers below.

At last the bells start to ring in the shrine and the drummers respond, picking up the strength and intensity of the previous nights' rhythm, pounding again so the earth shakes. The *dhāmi* bursts out through the crowded doorway, carrying his bells and a bronze bowl of turmeric-stained rice grains in one hand. He dances about among the crowd, greeting people here and there by stamping yellow rice marks on their foreheads with the thumb of his other hand.

The evening sun is low in the sky with its rays almost horizontal, piercing the *dhāmi*'s eyes as he turns back to face it. It tints his white tunic orange and projects his dancing shadow right back across the ground until it rises up with the juniper trunks.

He doesn't dance on his own for long. Soon two more *dhāmis* emerge from the shrine with their bells, and their heads bare and shaved bald except for their waist-length black tufts, braided at points with silver bands – gifts to the gods from their devotees. Then other *dhāmis*, immersed in the crowd, stand up shaking, jostling their neighbours and struggling to take off their jackets and their *topis* or turbans, and shoes if they have them. Two boys and a woman, who aren't even *dhāmis*, leap to their feet, possessed, their bodies spinning-tops set turning by the strength of the gods' will to dance.

A man from the audience is walking out among the dancers. He's wearing a garland of marigolds and carrying a bowl of yellow rice grains. He stops in the path of one of the dancing *dhāmis* and drapes the garland round his neck and plants a yellow *tīkā* between his eyes, greeting the god. The *dhāmi* stoops his head for the garland's embrace.

Other people follow suit and surge out into the space enclosed by the crowd. And as the *dhāmis* dance in the sunshine, the tiers of yellow garlands collide with their hair and bounce up and down against their white tunics. And there are flowers in their hair and loose yellow flowers strewn about under their bare feet on the ground.

> To test me the Bārakote king made me
> knead sand into a ball and made me carry

a load with rope made of stones. He
told me that if I had the power then I
could carry water to him in a basket.
And this I did. And then the king said,
'Now that you have shown me all that is
good, I wish to see all that is evil as
well.' I told him that I could do
anything, but that he would have to
suffer. Still he insisted that he
wanted to see all that is evil and he
forced me to prove my power.
So I brought about twenty-two earthquakes
and I caused that kingdom to tremble.
And when it had trembled for twenty-two
hours I told him that this glimpse
should be enough. I reasoned with him
in all manner of ways, but still he
wouldn't listen, So I shook the houses
and the palace and destroyed them and
caused the black-and-white snake demon to
fall from the skies, and stones and rocks
to fall from the skies. There was no
chance of survival. And then, when the
houses and palace were destroyed, the
floods came and washed everything away so
that you couldn't tell that this was this
place and that was that. Nothing could
be recognized.

Ten or twelve different gods are embodied now, and they are all amusing themselves in different ways. Some are dancing on their own, or in twos or threes, as they did in the moonlight. One is dancing his way round the outside of the shrine, carrying another sitting upright on his shoulder. It's the Bāhan, one of the demons the gods defeated in the past, who then reformed and became a lesser deity. Now he's restating his submission to the Bāra Bhāi and the forces of good.

47

There are others who aren't even dancing: one who has just gone over to the veranda and plunged his hand into the vat of boiling oil so he could offer a hot *puri* to a child in tears: another who is standing in the midst of the dancers being continually buffeted as they come and go, and hungrily eating a plateful of raw rice grains. When he's finished someone takes him some water and he drinks it, spilling it over his face and down his chest and bare legs and feet.

The crowd is delighted by the gods' high spirits and pleasure in the dance. People laugh and point as they recognize a particular god by his mannerisms, by the way he contorts the *dhāmi*'s body to dance, or smile, or leap high into the air. They've all come today: Bijulī Maṣṭā, Thārpā Bāhan, Ukhāri Maṣṭā, and Bhawāni the goddess, younger sister of the twelve Maṣṭā brothers. Even Yāṅgre has come, standing on his own with his back to the dancers, chewing marigold heads and squirting a jet of yellow pulp into a child's face. It cries out, horrified by the affront.

> There was a widow who came to me
> saying, 'There is no water in my land,
> so I have no rice to eat. My urine is
> like blood. I have come to ask for
> the gift of water.'
> And when she said this I struck the
> ground with my fist and water sprang out.
> I told that woman that if she offered me
> rice on the day of the transplanting
> there would always be water to flood her
> paddy fields.
> But because the woman was a widow and
> contemptible to other people, they
> rechannelled her water and she came to
> me weeping.
> So I destroyed that place to which the
> water had been taken and I cursed those

> people. I cursed those people and said
> that if ever they did scrape together
> some little wealth, then it would vanish
> like ice in water. I cursed those people
> and said that there would never be a
> single day when there wasn't someone ill
> in their house.

The sun sets and the harsh lines of sun and shadow dissolve into blurred shapes and muted colours. The *dhāmis* look almost human – as vulnerable as actors when the stagelights fail.

They carry on dancing, but they're only holding the attention of a small part of the audience. Most faces have turned to watch the *ḍāṅgri* who's just come out of the shrine and is standing in the doorway. He's wearing only a new white *dhoti* and his body looks old, its loose flesh striated with veins and sinews. In his right hand he's holding a curved knife with a short wooden handle.

He walks out of the shrine without looking at the crowd, picks up one of the lambs, frightened and bleating, and carries its almost weightless body round to the side of the shrine. He puts it down at the base of the new *liṅga* – the stripped pine trunk that all the men brought back from the forest and erected early this morning – and pours some water over the lamb's head and in a stripe down its back to the base of the tail. The lamb shrugs it off – nodding, they say, the god's acceptance and its own acquiescence – and the *ḍāṅgri* stoops down and saws through its throat. There's no resistance; it seems that the neck has no muscle, no bone, no leather hide, that it's just a blood-filled tube of white fur.

The *ḍāṅgri* holds the body while the young red blood squirts out and slashes the base of the *liṅga* in criss-cross patterns. When it has stopped coming, he drops the body and goes back for another lamb and another, creeping down the earthen steps with his blood-stained knife and his feet and ankles splashed with red.

He sacrifices four lambs at the base of the *liṅga*, then takes two

49

inside and kills them by slitting open the throat and the chest and cutting off one of the forelegs at the shoulder, so the heart can be taken out, still pumping, and offered to the god on a plate on the *dhāmi*'s raised seat.

The dancing has stopped now. All eyes have turned to the killing. And when the *ḍāṅgri* goes inside they remain fixed for an instant on the *liṅga* and the ground around it, with the four white bodies, and the separate wide-eyed heads, and the stains of blood going brown already in the trampled grass.

> In those days I brought about stability
> and made laws. If there was anyone who
> was suffering then I did whatever there
> was to be done and wiped away that
> person's tears. And if there was anyone
> who was causing suffering to others,
> then I would build a trap of poisoned
> bamboo, and I would ensnare and kill
> that person. I told them that I could
> do whatever I wanted – if I wished to
> do good, then it would be good and if I
> wished to do evil, then it would be evil.

Suddenly the crowd rearranges itself, like the changing pattern in a kaleidoscope; one twist and the border of any empty space dissolves into small agitating clusters spread throughout. There's a hiss of people talking and laughing, and the explosive shrieks of children playing, shaking off the intensity of the afternoon. A man is passing round some morsels of raw heart and liver. It's the *prasād*, food offered to the gods, eaten in essence and then passed back, blessed, for the people to eat.

The crowd lingers for a long time, until it's almost dark. There's a sense of release after the excitement, of fulfilment. The gods came; they ate and danced and then left contented. Now they're honour-bound to watch over the crops and the livestock and ward off ghosts and evil forces.

A group of men are standing on the veranda. They're calling out, one by one, the names of all the households in the village. Shapes move forward in the fading light to collect their pile of *puris*, the due from their offerings of flour and oil, and a few small pieces of meat, *prasād*.

> That place with its sweeping cedar trees
> and juniper. That place where I could be
> blessed by *Kaskā Sundari Devī* in the
> mornings and the evenings. There I built
> a shrine and sacrificed a he-goat in the
> name of the truth.
> If a bell is tied round the neck of a crow
> then, as it flies about, everyone will hear
> the ringing – so there was no one who did
> not know about the powers of this god. But
> mostly his influence was barely perceptible,
> like the blowing of a breeze, like the
> sound of a butterfly wafting through the
> air.

1. Kalchu.

2. A house in the village: the stables are at ground level, the
living quarters above, and a notched-pole ladder leads to the
roof-top work area and small storage room. On the hillside is a
Maṣṭā shrine.

3. Children swinging on the big walnut tree.

4. Sigarup, Hārkini and a pile of *lukals* filled with grain to be traded for salt at the Tibetan border.

5. Chola washing dishes.

6. Kalchu winnowing, with Patrāsi Himal in the background.

7. Jakali shovelling snow from the roof of her house.

8. The *ḍāṅgri*'s daughter, Gaiḍi, smoking a *chillim*.

FOUR SEASONS WITH THE SHEEP

WHEN THE GODS WERE ASKED TO NAME AN AUSPICIOUS DAY FOR the sheep to go south to Aula for the six months of winter, they had said the twenty-second of Kārtik, November the sixth. The night before, Kalchu and Sigarup went to the shrine, lit the oil lamp and tied two strips of new cloth – one red, one white – on to the rafters among the hundreds of old and blackened ones that had gathered there over the years. It was as if those streamers, knotted to the shrine, ensured the gods' protection – that Bhawāni, who went south, would bring the shepherds safely home again and Maiyu would take care of all those who stayed behind; as if the streamers knotted autumn safely on to spring.

Before it was light Chola had lit a fire, and was frying *puris* and boiling a small pan of rice for Sigarup to eat before he left. By dawn the room was full of people. Murti Lāl and Māilo,* Sigarup's cousin and uncle who were joining their flocks with Kalchu's for the journey, had come to check the final preparations. Other male relatives dropped in to offer last-minute words of advice, or simply wish the party well. Some had brought instructions for things they wanted from the bazaars. Money changed hands. Voices buzzed, then rose in laughter or to make a point more forcibly.

Kalchu and Sigarup were only half-attending. They were busy packing a basket with the things that Sigarup would need, talking quietly, moving back and forth between the two rooms; collecting blankets, cooking pots, a bag of wheat flour, salt and chilli, the cotton tarpaulin that they stretched across upright sticks to make a tent.

When at last they sat down to eat, a small crowd of children had gathered in the doorway, drawn from their own homes by the smell of *puris* frying, knowing from this that today was a

* See Glossary.

special occasion. Jakali shooed them away as she came in. She'd brought some *desu*, flat buckwheat bread that's taken on journeys because it stays fresh for days, and some roasted amaranthus seeds in honey, wrapped in birch bark. She put them into the basket and Chola stretched across the fire to pass her a *puri*.

They brought the whole flock of sheep and goats, thirty-five or forty of them, on to the roof to tie on the *lukals* – the double-pouched woven saddle-bags – stuffed with potatoes and Tibetan salt for trading in the south. Śaṅkar and Kānchho* were down below steering them out of the sheep-pen, round and up the wide stone staircase. Kāli and her cousin, Jit, were at the far end of the roof waving their arms, keeping the sheep contained at one end only, stopping them going back down the steps at the other side.

Hooves clattered on the stone stairway as the sheep bounded up two abreast, then more hollowly on the packed mud roof. The first ones ran straight over to the corner of the roof, saw the drop and veered back, colliding with the others still pouring up the staircase. Frightened now, hemmed into the confined space with no escape, they ran in unison, a few steps one way, then the other, heads thrown back above the shifting bodies, yellow eyes ablaze.

Kalchu grabbed hold of a ram that was panting on the outside of the flock. He clutched it by two handfuls of thick fleece, bracing himself as it tried to lunge forwards. Then quickly he put one leg over the body, gripping the shoulders between his thighs and the ram stood still, its head drooping sullenly. Sigarup passed a *lukal*, and Kalchu slung it over the ram's back and tied the two sets of strings, one across the chest and the other round the hind legs and under the tail.

When he let it go the ram trotted off, barging through the other sheep with the *lukal* bulging out on either side across its ribcage. It stopped abruptly at the edge of the roof, straining to balance its top-heavy body on slender back legs and egg-cup hooves.

* See Glossary.

Chola and Mina were watching from the doorway with the twins hovering behind, peering out, both curious and scared by the rush of trampling hooves. Nara was perched safely halfway up the notched-pole ladder to the upper roof. He seemed completely absorbed, his whole body thrilled with excitement.

When the sheep were calmer, Kalchu and Sigarup waded out among them, slapping rumps, pushing hard against firmly resistant flanks, piling the already packed bodies tighter together so there was more room to move about with the *lukals*.

By the time all the *lukals* had been tied on Murti Lāl and Māilo were waiting down below, their flocks merged together quietly grazing. Kāli and Jit moved out of the way of the back staircase and the sheep flooded down past them. Kalchu followed behind, raising his arms and whistling at the stragglers. He would go with them at least as far as the bridge.

Sigarup picked up the basket, staggering slightly to readjust the weight, and Chola came out of the doorway with a bowl of rice-grains stained with turmeric. She dipped her thumb into the bowl and then touched Sigarup's forehead, marking a yellow *ṭikā* between his eyes. Sigarup bowed his head and cupped both palms loosely in front of his face, as if none of the yellow rice should fall to the ground. Afterwards he dipped his own thumb into the bowl and made the same yellow mark on Chola's forehead. Then he turned and was gone.

Chola reached up to the arch above the doorway and seven times made the same imprint with the pad of her thumb on to seven discs of semi-dried cow-dung. Then, with her back to the door, she sprinkled the rest of the contents of the bowl high into the air and out over the edge of the roof.

At the end of November, ten or eleven boys climbed the big walnut tree in the middle of the village, swinging about among its branches, and women and children scrabbled laughingly for the nuts as they fell. Soon afterwards a wind sent the last of its bright leaves spiralling down.

One stormy evening in December a party of Tibetan traders drove their yaks down the steep path into the village from the west. They were silhouetted for a moment on the brow of the hill against a last pool of light among encroaching black storm-clouds. They walked in a line, the yaks' bulky bodies braced against the wind, tails streaming out. Then they rounded the bend by the Bāhan shrine and dropped down into the darkness of the valley. They set up camp on the Kālādika, unloading the yaks and lighting a fire as the moon rose low behind the trees.

They stayed for two weeks, grazing the yaks. One of the bulls had been bitten by a wildcat one night, on a mountain pass coming down from Dolpo. The wound had become infected by the constant rubbing of a heavy load. The flesh had had to be gouged out with a knife, and the wound swilled with water and coated with powdered herbs. Three men held the yak's head down with ropes, their weight pitted against the great muscles of its neck and shoulders as it threw its head about, crazy with the pain of the knife in its withers.

Early one morning they tied their stripy woven bags of Tibetan salt on to the yaks and left for the south. Their fires were still curling blue smoke into the frosty air as they filed out of the village and across the icy boards of the small bridge.

In January the first real snow fell. Kāli stood outside and shouted, '*Hiuṅ āyo!*' and, tilting her head back, mouth open wide, watched the flakes fall about her and felt them melt like icy duck-down on the warmth of her outstretched tongue.

For two days nothing beyond the ghost of the walnut tree showed through the flickering screen of brownish-yellow light.

On the third morning a gust of wind swept out one final flurry and cleared the sky. Kalchu, Nara and Kāli fetched the wooden shovels and, standing thigh-high in the snow, set about the long work of clearing the roof. Right across the village, men and women stooped over, black forms against a world of white, shovelling great heaps of snow and tumbling them to the ground in frothy white cascades.

It was snowing again, or sleeting, when Kalchu's uncle died in February. They bound his small and wizened body in a white cloth and two grown sons carried it out of the house on a pair of pine poles resting almost weightlessly between their four strong shoulders. They took it down to the burning *ghaṭ* where two rivers meet in a rolling pool of green and white, and where at night the restless spirits of the dead wail to the roar of the crashing waters.

Chola and Mina stood on the roof and watched them go. The dead man was taken at the end of a winding procession, with one man from every house in the village barefoot and carrying a log for the pyre. A long white strip of cloth linked them all from hand to hand as they made their way down through the sleet and the open snowy fields.

Later the women saw the smoke billowing up from the river valley.

When Kalchu came back his head had been shaved bald except for a short black tuft that arched out from the crown and drooped down behind. He complained of the cold and started to wear a thick cotton turban instead of his usual *ṭopi*.

For ten days in March the water-mills froze solid. The stream cascaded down, spangling sunlight on ice-capped rocks and luminous green weed, but the chutes were blocked and the water passed them by. The supplies of flour ran out.

One night Mina and Kāli went to use the Chaura mill. They wrapped themselves up in thick woollen blankets and, laden with a sack of grain and a bundle of firewood, set out across the darkness. They lit a fire in the stone mill-hut and all night huddled round it, spooning ladles of pale maize kernels into the central well of the grinding stone. Outside the water churned down beneath them, pumping the mechanism, clashing wood against stone, stone against heavily-spinning grinding-stone.

At dawn they ate the potatoes that they'd laid around the fire to cook. Kāli swept up the drifts of flour and, scooping it up in her limply cold hands, crammed it back into the bag. Later the Chaura women came to use their mill.

March ended and a web of green enlaced the thorn trees. One day, instead of the usual austere frost and intensely clear light as dawn subsided, the air felt thick and warm. A band of cloud stretched low across the valley and it was raining slightly. In the distance the pine-clad hills were bathed in a pale wash of greenish-purple light. Groups of Tibetan traders filed through the village on their way back north from India. Local men returned from their winter working in Jumla Bazaar.

Kalchu finished weaving the last whitish length of woollen cloth to make a jacket and put his loom away. The following morning he brought the two black bulls out of the stable and went to start the ploughing. When he came back in the evening he sat for a long time gazing out across the V-shaped valley leading south. 'If they don't get back by *Chait Dasain* – if Bhawāni's not here for her own festival – it's a bad sign. It'll be a bad year for us all.'

One day, on his way to do the ploughing, he met a man who'd just come back from the south and had passed several flocks of sheep on the other side of Chhakuri Lekh. He said that the rain we'd been having here had fallen as snow on the top of the pass. There was a terrible wind blowing as well, sheeting across the plateau, piling the snow into drifts as high as a house. He said that one group had foolishly tried to cross and sixteen sheep had been lost – some swept right off the path as they climbed to the top, some left injured or dead, buried in snow at the bottom of a hidden ravine. The other groups had set up camp on the far side, waiting for a few clear days and the worst of the snow to melt. It was bitter, he said, so cold you thought your eyelids would freeze shut if you blinked.

Days passed. In spare moments Kalchu and Chola would pause on the roof, anxiously scanning the valley from length to breadth, up and down.

Then one evening Kalchu spotted some sheep, a moving patch of white, away in the distance between Māthichaur and Gorigāuṅ, slowly working its way down the valley. There were three figures with them, black hazy shadows that swayed in and out of focus and occasionally flickered away to nothing. Everyone rushed out when he called, screwing up their faces, trying to hold their vision steady long enough to tell if it was Sigarup. But no one could do more than guess ... and hope. Kalchu put on his jacket and hurried down the path towards the bridge.

It was almost dark when the sheep squeezed through the narrow path between two houses and spilled out across the open village square. There must have been a hundred of them – three flocks together – scrabbling over the stones, stretching out their necks and bleating. Sigarup and Murti Lāl followed the last few through the gap, whistling long and low, a final command to stop and be still.

When Sigarup climbed up the ladder, straining under the weight of his basket, the dog sidled over to him with a low unearthly grunt of pleasure. Hārkini rushed over and wrapped both arms round his thigh, burying her face deep in the folds of his matted wool trousers. Chola, reaching up, replaced the seven yellow marks above the doorway with seven new ones and then, facing Sigarup almost shyly, she planted three *ṭikās* firmly between his eyes. Sigarup stooped and touched her feet.

Shafts of bright sunlight pierced the smoke as it welled up from the eaves and spread across the roof in a fine blue film. Kāli came out into the doorway with a plate of *puris* and a small bowl of oil. The bronze plate caught the sun and flashed its glinting radiance back across her face. She gathered up her skirt and climbed the notched-pole ladder to the shrine on the upper roof. Inside she put the *puris* down on the altar for Bhawāni and Maiyu and lit the lamp. Sunlight filtered dustily through the slats of the door and dimmed its flame. At night it would shine out brightly, projecting the shrine's own life back in wavering shadows across the walls and ceiling.

Afterwards the gods' *puris* were torn up and shared out as *prasād*. There were more *puris* – a whole basketful – eaten with hot spicy potatoes, fried in mustard oil brought back from Aula, and there was rice for everyone, and an emerald green soup of wild young *kankani* leaves. Kalchu had brewed some millet beer months ago to ferment out ready for today and it was sweet and clear and very strong.

Hārkini and Lāla Bahādur were lolling happily against Sigarup's knees, chattering incoherently as he started to unpack the basket. There was cloth – yards and yards of *tetua*, cheap and coarsely woven cotton – and a shawl, finely printed in yellow and black, the kind that all the village women wear at festivals. There were *chillims* – one rupee for seven. There were brightly coloured *topis*, a cigarette lighter and a set of batteries for the radio. There were spices – a small cloth pouch of cumin and a bigger one of turmeric.

Kāli and Hārkini were huddled together in the corner of the room where sunlight flooded through the open doorway. Kāli had fixed two new hairslides on either side of Hārkini's head and was holding her face at arm's length to see the effect. The slides were white and round with protruding domes of multicoloured plastic. Tilting Hārkini's head to catch the sun, Kāli angled the reflection on to the wall, casting a stained-glass disc of red, yellow, green, blue and orange circles – splaying it back and forth across the wall according to the movements of her sister's head.

She herself had plastic bangles. They were multicoloured too, but not clear and translucent like the hairslides. They were cloudy colours, pale and subtle with the milky sheen of pearls. She squeezed them painfully, one after the other, over her hand. When all five were in place she raised her arm, and smiled, admiring them.

For a moment there was a quietness, everyone reflecting. Then Sigarup sat up and pulled a large lemon out of his pocket. Its rind was like wide-pored skin, shining greasily. He cut it up lengthways and its tangy smell flooded out. After he'd coated the segments in salt and chilli he passed them round, and everyone smacked their lips and screwed up their faces in pained delight. He told them about the oranges and bananas that grow in Aula and the quantities of milk and curd, and then about the monkeys that hop around and eat the crops.

Kalchu stood up. There was work to do. He folded up the cloth: the *tetua*; the length of saffron satin to enwind his own or Chola's body when they died; the yards and yards of white muslin funeral cloth; and finally the *pheṭā* and *pachyauro* – turban and shawl – ritual gifts that, one day, Sigarup would give to the parents of the girl he'd marry. He put them all away in the big wooden chest. Then he told Kāli to go and graze the cows, and Biḍā to tend the sheep. Reluctantly they left.

Outside Sigarup and Kalchu started to unpack the *lukals*, slitting open the stitching at the top with a knife and tipping out the maize to dry in the sun before they stored it away in wooden chests and cylindrical clay grain vats. Later, some of it would be loaded up again and taken north to trade for salt.

When all the grain had been spread out on every kind of tattered rug and mat that the house possessed, it stretched out almost right across the roof. They had to pile it deeper in one corner to make a space to spread the chillies – five *lukals* of fleshy scarlet pods to be dried a crackling brick-red to last throughout the year.

At last they slumped down in the sunshine with two long bamboos to chase away the chickens. Other men and children, mainly relatives, gathered round and Kalchu fetched the beer. All through the afternoon they sat and drank and talked about the trip. Sigarup said that three sheep had died – there was some disease. Kalchu laughed and, teasing him, asked how much he had sold them for. Then they discussed the exchange rate: one of salt to five of grain, better than the year before. But the price of *tetua* had rocketed because of the increased land tax in the villages that made it. Kalchu picked up a handful of maize kernels, inspected them for a minute, and let them trickle back through his fingers. He said the quality seemed good.

Towards evening the tailor came. Sitting outside surrounded by the family, he unfurled rolls and rolls of cotton cloth and, pulling it taut, he measured it with string – a jacket for Chola, trousers for Sigarup and Nara, and an all-in-one toddler suit for Lāla Bahādur. He marked the material with charcoal, cut it into lengths, and rolled it up again. Chola fetched him some tobacco and a parcel of turmeric. Later, when he brought the finished clothes back, he'd be paid in grain.

Two months later spring had opened into full-blown summer. The lambing had begun and the sheep's tousled fleece had been shorn to a jagged grey stubble.

When the rains came Sigarup took the flock to the monsoon settlement to graze the mountain pastures. They left in the early morning, swishing through the wet grass on the valley floor, then climbing steeply into the thick of the mist and cloud.

In August Kalchu began to fill the *lukals*, stuffing them with maize and barley, then sliding a knife between the grain and the cloth so the contents would settle and more could be crammed on top. When they were bulging-full, he stitched them closed with a curved needle and woollen thread and laid them ready in a pile.

One evening Sigarup brought the rams and he-goats down from the mountain pastures and Śaṅkar went to take his place, tending the ewes and lambs.

The following morning they lit the oil-lamp in the shrine and loaded up the sheep. Sigarup and Murti Lāl exchanged *ṭikās* with their families and, whistling and shouting, they steered the flock through the village and out across the bridge. Slowly they worked their way up the wide and gently rising river-valley until they were black sticks bent against their baskets of provisions. At last they were lost from sight, merging with the river and the pine trees and the foothills of the looming mountain ridges leading northwards to Tibet.

They didn't get as far as the Tibetan border, where the exchange rate would have been better. Twenty-eight days later they were back – they had only been as far as Mugu. They had stayed there with their *iṣṭa*, the trading partner whose family had done business with Kalchu's since before his grandfather could remember. They bartered their grain for the salt he'd brought back from the border, where he traded with Tibetans who'd scraped it from the arid salt-lakes and carried it south on yaks across the windswept dust-blown plateau lands.

Soon after he returned Sigarup took the rams and he-goats back to the mountain pastures. He spent one more month in that makeshift hut, grazing the sheep and gathering *hātijaro*, *balṭu* and *katuka* – wild herbs – to sell as medicine in Aula. The rains were over now and the lambs were almost grown. When the first frosts came he moved back down to the village. Then, in a seance, one cold and perfectly clear starlit night, the gods were asked to name the day to go to Aula.

WHEN SIGARUP FELL ILL

SIGARUP HAD BEEN ILL FOR A WEEK. NO ONE KNEW WHAT WAS wrong. He had a fever and complained about a pain in his right thigh.

By the ninth day the pain had become intolerable. All through the night he lay awake, twisting and writhing, and moaning in low desperate tones. Kalchu sat up with him, keeping the fire alight, while the rest of the family slept. Occasionally he would mutter a few words of comfort, or reach out a hand and lay it reassuringly on Sigarup's blanketed body to let him know that he was still awake. But most of the night he sat in silence, gazing abstractedly into the fire.

In the morning Chola said that she too was feeling unwell. When she went to fetch the water she felt sharp pains rushing through her body. She was gasping for air, then her throat seized closed and she fainted. Kalchu spoke to the *dhāmi* and asked him to call the god to the shrine that night.

When darkness had fallen, Biḍā and Saṅkar climbed the ladder to the upper roof of Kalchu's house and brought the two copper kettledrums out of the shrine at the back. Wrapped in thick blankets against the cold, they sat cross-legged behind the drums, beating them in unison, and the sound rolled out through the frosty night, letting the villagers know that the god would be coming.

Inside the shrine three men sat around the fire. One of them was Kalchu, who had come early to make sure of a place at the front before the small shrine filled up with people. Another was the *ḍaṅgri*, sitting beside a petal-shaped oil lamp which he replenished as soon as the flame began to dwindle from a bowl on the hearth. The third, dressed in white, was the *dhāmi*. They were talking quietly, waiting for people to arrive.

The shrine itself seemed to be waiting. There was a strange

stillness in the air. The fire was burning almost smokelessly, with just a thin trail of white projected vertically above the shifting peaks of orange flame. The smell of juniper, burned earlier as incense, still lingered like the warm breath of the forest in summer. Outside the open door stretched the immense blackness of night.

Soon people began to arrive, taking off their shoes outside the door, peeling back shawls and blankets from faces that glowed red with the cold. Children fidgeted and chattered; mothers clutched babies in their arms and hauled toddlers on to their laps, making more room on the floor for people to sit. Everyone had brought a small handful of husked rice, which they passed to the front to be put on a plate beside the *dhāmi*.

When the shrine was full, Kalchu began to pull the cord of the big brass bell hanging above his head. The bell swung round, clanging and reverberating. Like the sound of a gong, it was impossible to tell where the clash of the clapper on the bell ended and its echo began. A continuous multi-pitched hum whirred deafeningly around the shrine.

Outside on the roof the drummers began to speed up, thrashing the great cavernous half-globes as fast as their hands could rise and fall. The shrine and the whole house shook and the ground beneath it seemed to be shifting away as though in an earthquake. It was a demoniac sound that made hearts beat too fast, heads and bodies reel.

The *dhāmi* was sitting cross-legged with his eyes closed. Then, suddenly, he began to tremble. His breath was coming in short irregular gasps. Occasionally, as if he was trying to control it, he would exhale three times in succession, and the sound would be forced from his throat in rhythmic grunts: 'Aha aha aha'. Then, lurching to his feet, he moved over on to the only empty seat in the shrine – a patch of floor covered with a sheepskin rug. There he pulled off his white turban and let his long black hair coil over his shoulder and drop down on to the ground. The music stopped. For an instant its echo lingered. Then there was silence.

The *dhāmi* put his hand into the plate of rice, agitating the grains, stirring them round, picking them up, then letting them sift back through his fingers. For a long time he gazed into the depths of the rice, muttering. Streams of words, too fast and tremulous to understand, poured from his mouth in the voice of the god. Then the grunts came again: 'Aha aha aha', and the muttering continued.

At last, with his hand still shuffling the rice, he looked up, directly at Kalchu. 'Child, your eyes are full of suffering.'

'Lord, there is illness in my family. My son is dying. You must help me now. I've lived a good life. I've honoured the gods and cared for my family. Tell me: if this is the punishment from you or another god for something I have done that's wrong then show me how to make amends. I'll do anything, if only my son is spared. Or if this is the whim of some trouble-stirring witch, you must beat her to the ground and punish her. Make her stop. That you owe me, Lord, as a man who's always worshipped you.'

There was silence for a minute. Then the god's voice came again and Kalchu leaned forward, straining to hear. 'Child, I see no witch and nothing you have done that's wrong. But listen, if you lived a nomad's life wandering the high mountains you would understand. Looking up at the north-facing slope ahead you would see snow and ice and you would tremble, but you would know that coming down on the other side, you would walk in sunshine, through green grass and sweet-smelling flowers. Don't you know that in your life too there are mountains and there are valleys? Times of trouble come and go – that is our lot.'

'But my son – you must save my son. If this son dies my life is finished. I'll do anything. I'll give you anything you want.' Kalchu was distraught.

'Child, listen to me. Your son may live, or he may die. But remember this: even if he dies, better times will come for you. I will not see you suffering for long. Trust in me and I will guide you through.'

The *dhāmi* picked up a handful of rice and blew on it. Then he passed it to Kalchu. 'Take these grains as my blessing. Tonight, scatter half into the wind to the north, the south, the east and the west. Then give the rest to the boy to eat.'

There was a buzz of voices in the shrine. A man beside Kalchu turned and spoke to him encouragingly. *Chillims* were lit and passed around. The *dhāmi* was staring at the ground, blinking rapidly and trembling. Beside him a three-pronged trident was staked into the low altar, and next to that a jumble of miniature statues danced with their shadows in the firelight. There were men on horseback, sentries with their guns, a cow being milked, a woman with round breasts and her hair coiled with snakes. To the left of them, a conch shell brought back from the Indian Ocean curled mysteriously in on itself, like the pink and white entrance to another world.

Then the god spoke to a woman whose baby was ill, and afterwards to a couple who were childless after three years' marriage. He told the woman she was a witch and was holding her husband under a strange and evil power. The woman said it was not true and the god asked her why she had come tonight if she thought that his words were 'mere wind and breeze'. She relented and the god said that if she sacrificed a chicken at the Bāhan shrine on top of the hill, that god would exorcize her evil. She started to cry.

While he was still talking to that woman, the *dhāmi*'s body slowly began to relax. He was no longer shaking. His eyes had lost their glazed intensity and the fits of rapid blinking had stopped. Then calmly, in a voice that was his own, he said that the god had left him.

A cold breeze blew through the open door, stirring the fire so the flames shot up, flickering brightly. For a moment, the tangle of small brass bells and strips of red and white cloth hanging from the roof were illuminated, then they were plunged back into darkness.

The *dhāmi* picked up his long tuft of hair bound with silver rings that had been given to the god he embodied, and carefully wound it round his head again and covered it with his turban.

After the god had left, most people stayed in the shrine discussing what had been said. When the light and warmth of the fire had given way to smoke, they put on their shoes and wandered homeward through the silent village and the frosty starlit night.

The next morning Chola seemed to be slightly better but Sigarup, if anything, was worse. All day he lay in the dark windowless room, semi-conscious. In the evening Chola woke him with some water to drink; he winced and then groaned as the pain shot out from his thigh and radiated through his body. For a moment his eyes looked at her beseechingly, then they clouded over and were vacant. He slouched back under his rug.

That night Kalchu's two brothers came to look at Sigarup, and the three men and Chola sat around the fire discussing in low worried voices what they were going to do. In the end Kalchu and Chola agreed that Sigarup would have to go to the hospital in Jumla Bazaar. Kānchho, Kalchu's younger brother, and Śaṅkar would take him in the morning, and Kānchho would stay there with him – if that was how it had to be.

All that night again Kalchu kept his vigil. Then, at the first light of dawn, the three men began their preparations while Chola cooked. Together they cut a section out of a basket, from the broad rim right down to the narrower base. The gap was about a foot and a half wide – wide enough for Sigarup to sit in the basket with his legs hanging down below. When it was ready, they padded it with straw and blankets. Then they packed another basket with some *roṭis* for the journey, and flour and potatoes and pots and pans for cooking when they reached the Bazaar.

After they had eaten, Kalchu picked up Sigarup in his blanket, holding the limp body draped across his two forearms as he would a child. Gently, he carried him outside and put him in the basket.

Kalchu, Chola, Nara, Kāli and the twins stood on the roof and watched them go. The two men were dressed in their best clothes for the Bazaar, with Sigarup, pale and lifeless, looking out back-

wards from the shrouds of his blanket in the basket on Kānchho's
back. As they went down the steps, Sigarup's face contorted at
the sudden jarring movements. Kalchu's eyes filled with tears,
and Chola, holding her face in both her hands, was racked with
sobbing.

Late the following afternoon, Śaṅkar came back. He said that the
doctor seemed to think Sigarup would be all right – although his
chances would have been better if they'd brought him sooner. He
had an infection of the muscle and would have to stay in hospital
for at least three weeks, maybe a month, while they treated him
with penicillin injections.

Later in the evening, when the sheep and cows were in, and
the family was sitting round the fire, Śaṅkar told them the whole
story of what had happened.

'It seemed that we would never reach the Bazaar. Although
Sigarup's so thin now, it was a difficult weight to carry and we
needed to rest a lot. Then his leg began to hurt and we had to
stop to rearrange the straw and blanket. In the woods between
Lāmri and Uṭhu where the path drops steeply down, the stream
had frozen solid right across the path and we had to pick our way
for half a mile, across the ice.

'We didn't make it to the Bazaar last night. We stayed in the
dharamsālā, just past Uṭhu. Although we found some firewood in
the woods behind the hut, it was bitterly cold. None of us really
slept; we just lay there, listening to the wind and the jackals
howling.

'We got to the Bazaar soon after the sun was up this morning.
There was already a crowd of people sitting on the grass outside
the hospital. The doctor hadn't arrived yet, but another man
wrote down Sigarup's name and village and told us to wait.

'It was midday when Sigarup's name was called. We went
into a room and the doctor asked some questions and looked at
Sigarup's leg and felt it. Then he told us to go into the hospital
where the nurse would show us what to do.

'The hospital was dark and cold and there were two rows of beds, six on either side. The nurse pointed to a bed in the corner where Sigarup would sleep, and another, next to it, for Kānchho Ba. She took Sigarup's temperature and gave him an injection and some pills. Then she told us that there was a hut behind the hospital where the patients lit a fire and cooked their food.

'Inside, a boy was sitting by the fire. The hut was filled with smoke. He said that he'd been there three weeks. He had tuberculosis and was getting better slowly. But it wasn't easy. In his valley the ploughing's started and, because his family's small, no one could be spared to come with him to help him fetch his wood and water – and although the water's nearby, the firewood's half a day away.

'He was glad that Sigarup had come, because up to now he'd been the only patient staying and, alone at night, he was terrified of ghosts – of the restless souls of all the people who must have died there, far from their homes and families.'

Chola winced visibly at this, and Śaṅkar carried on. 'We made ourselves some *roṭis*, and when we'd eaten them, I set out for home. Kānchho Ba says you mustn't worry – he'll stay with Sigarup however long it takes him to get better.' Then he added, 'If anyone from the village is going to the Bazaar we should send some more flour and potatoes and some more blankets.'

In the days and weeks that followed, Chola was sometimes well, sometimes ill. She complained of headaches and exhaustion and often said her whole body ached. Sometimes she thought she had a fever and, in the morning when she'd cooked and the family had eaten, too ill to work in the fields, she'd take a rug out onto the roof and sleep in the warmth of the winter sun.

Kalchu was busy all the time, working the land from dawn to dusk. First he did the ploughing in both his own fields and Kānchho's. Then as spring advanced, he sowed the barley, millet, potatoes and the maize – his own and Kānchho's.

One day he didn't work. Early in the morning, dressed in his best clothes – his blue cotton tunic and trousers and his Chinese canvas shoes – he left to go to Chaura to consult one of the Chaura village gods. Another day he went to Gorigāuṅ, then further to Padmāra and to Rini. But always, coming back, he would be disconsolate. Always the message was the same: 'Child, I could set fire to green grass, but it would not burn.' The gods saw no solution and were steadfast in denying him the solace of their lies.

Then, late one afternoon when Chola had been ill for three consecutive days, Kalchu asked the *dhāmi* once again to call the god to the shrine on the roof of his own house.

The drumming began and Kalchu went to the shrine with his handful of husked rice, a red and a white strip of cotton cloth and a small bell to give to the god.

Again the music rang out and the god answered the summons. In the flickering firelight Kalchu beseeched him, 'Lord, you are the one who, when we have nothing, feeds us with water and clothes us with the wind. Help me now.'

That afternoon the floor of the shrine had been freshly plastered with mud and cow-dung and was smooth and clean, and the hearth had been cleared of its old ash. The fire was burning steadily, the flame of the oil-lamp dipped and bobbed and the sweet smell of incense filled the air. In that quiet order the god replied, 'Child, there is a woman. There is a woman, your wife. Many years ago she was married to a man in Lāmri. Then, when she met you she fell in love and wanted to come and live with you. In those hard times she turned to the god in the village where she lived, and that god stood by her. That god stood by both of you. You paid her husband three thousand rupees and you took away his wife.

'Now you have five sons. You have crops that flourish in the fields. You have cattle in your stable and a flock of sheep. But you have neglected that god. Now your wife is ill, and your son too may die. Tomorrow you must go the shrine of that god in Lāmri and sacrifice a he-goat. Then, once every three years, on the full moon in Kārtik, you will remember that god and you will offer him a lamb.'

The *dhāmi* blew on a handful of rice and passed it to Kalchu.

'Take these grains as my blessing, and may your days be as bright and continuous as a garland of flowers.'

The following morning Chola dressed in her best clothes: her blue printed cotton skirt, a freshly washed white waistband, a clean shawl and a pair of canvas shoes. Kalchu went down to the stable and selected a he-goat. Together the two of them set out for Lāmri, leading the goat on a length of rope.

When they came back, soon after midday, Chola was in good spirits. The goat had been sacrificed at the shrine and the meat shared out among the villagers. They had stayed to eat with the family of Chola's former husband, and they had been feasted with *raksi* and rice and the meat of the sacrificial goat.

The next day Chola was feeling well, and she and Kalchu and Kānchho's wife, Sita, worked in the fields all day and finished sowing the buckwheat. In the evening Kalchu went round the village from house to house until he found someone who was going to the Bazaar the following day. He asked them to bring back news of Sigarup and to take some flour and potatoes and a small parcel of rice grains blessed by the god.

Word came back in two days' time that Sigarup was getting better.

Soon afterwards another message came. Sigarup was setting out for home. He could walk now with a crutch, but the going would be slow, and they would spend the night in Lorpa.

The journey took them two full days. They left the hospital in the morning, and they didn't reach the village until the following evening.

As soon as they were back the room filled up with people: Kānchho's wife and family, Kalchu's other brother, Māilo, and his son and daughter, the *ḍaṅgri* from the house next door. When everyone was sitting round the fire, drinking beer and asking

Sigarup about his leg, about the doctor and the hospital and the journey back, Kalchu disappeared outside.

The night was cold, the frost already settling. There was a new moon, and its pale light cast soft shadows in the stillness. Kalchu went to the chicken coop and lifted the hatch. As he put his hand inside there was a squawking and a scrabbling of claws and flapping wings. Eventually he found the cockerel and pulled it out. Feathers flurried to the ground as it struggled in his hands.

To the west of the village across the stream, at the point where two paths meet, there is a small shrine. Two stones, standing vertically, mark the spot. Above them, tied to a thorn tree, faded red and white streamers dangle like the tattered carcasses of scrawny birds.

Holding the cockerel between his knees, Kalchu slit its throat. Then he lifted the body so that the blood dribbled over the stones and spilt on to the ground in front of him, where it was littered with the remains of other, older offerings – dead flowers, grains of rice and barley, a few coins.

Late that night there was a feast of rice and meat.

Two weeks later Sigarup was still weak. He couldn't stand or walk alone and the muscle in his leg had withered badly. But his face was full and there was colour in his cheeks. He talked and laughed a lot, and practised walking with his crutch. Every day he rubbed some ointment on his leg. It was red and smelled of perfume. He'd bought it in the Bazaar from an Indian trader who told him it would make the muscle grow.

In the month of Sāun, Kalchu and Sigarup set out together across the mountains on a pilgrimage to Rānāmāche Lake. On the night of the full moon, people gathered there from as far afield as Bārakot, twelve days' walk away. In the moonlight they bathed in the lake and made offerings to the goddess Rānāmāche Mai. There were people there whose parents, brothers, sisters, husbands – loved ones – had died in the course of the last year. Standing on the edge of the lake, they threw some small memento of their dead into the rippling water – a final request that their souls should rest in peace. And there were others, like Kalchu and Sigarup, who'd come instead to thank the gods for the life they'd spared.

PHASES OF THE MONSOON

ONE MORNING EARLY IN JUNE, BETWEEN DAWN AND SUNRISE, THE headman stood on his roof and shouted out across the village that today they would build the temporary bridge over the main river and that one man from each household was needed.

Thirty or so men left together and others followed in smaller groups throughout the morning. They crossed the river on the permanent bridge, couched solidly well above the water level on great wooden pillars carved at the top into the heads and shoulders of semi-mythical sentries, some holding rifles. On the far side they followed the river about a mile downstream until they reached the same narrow point where the temporary bridge is constructed every year. Here they left the valley and climbed up into the forest.

It took them all day to build the bridge – felling two of the tallest pines, stripping them bare, easing them with ropes down the steep slope to the river. Some of the men undressed to their loincloths and waded out into the cold water while others pushed the trees from the bank.

Although at this time of year, before the monsoon, the water is at its lowest, it was nevertheless chest-deep in places and fast-flowing – turquoise and white where it swirled around boulders near the edge, dark green in the broad sweep of the central canal. It was hard for the men not to lose their footing on jagged or slippery stones; harder still, leaning right back on the ropes, to counteract the relentless downward pull of the current and keep the tree on course for the opposite bank.

When both trunks had been hauled on to the far bank they used the ropes to bind them together at various points along their length. Finally they wedged the ends in place between boulders and the bridge was complete.

All the next day, women filed back and forth across the bridge carrying basketloads of *mal* – the manured pine-needle bedding from the cow-byres of last year's monsoon settlements on Jimale – to spread on the paddy fields directly opposite. When the baskets were full the women couldn't look down; their heads were braced erect by the tension of the rope across their foreheads bearing the weight of the load on their backs. But coming back, even with the baskets empty, they looked ahead not down, knowing that the sight of the water surging past only inches below their feet would have cost them their balance.

By the evening of the third day the cow-byres had been cleared and the paddy fields were dotted with deposited *mal* like chains of molehills.

Two weeks later the monsoon started; the river swelled under the double overload of heavy rain and melted snow from the mountains. Soon it was wild and tumultuous, crashing in on itself, rolling and somersaulting into frothing white whirlpools and eddies, roaring out across the valley like the rumble of an interminable train. The temporary bridge was first of all submerged then, like a matchstick, it was lifted up and swept aside.

It had been raining all night and in the stillness of morning the clouds and mist had not yet cleared. From the edge of the village the whole valley – the fields, the growing crops, the river – had been transformed into a steaming white nether-world. Mountains on the other side of the valley rose from the mist like islands, and here and there flecks of cloud, as pale and fine as sea-spray, trailed across their sombre, wooded slopes.

Mina was the first to leave for the fields. She joined a group of young women, each wrapped in a shawl and carrying a short-handled hoe for weeding and a smouldering disc of dried cow-dung to ward off the midges that plague the mornings and evenings of the rainy season. They picked their way slowly through the mud and puddles on the village path, unfurling a haze of blue smoke around them as they went.

Later, when they had eaten, Kalchu and Chola, Nara and the twins followed. Chola was carrying a basket with the hoes and a rug, some *roṭis* to eat in the course of the day and a bronze pot for fetching water from the spring. Kalchu was carrying Lāla Bahādur on his back in a shawl and gently coaxing Hārkini along by the hand.

When they had left the village, passing beneath the clump of wild apricot trees, bespattered with blossom, they walked in single file between the fields. Grass and tangled weeds criss-crossed the path, slashing their bare feet and ankles and saturating the clothes on their thighs where they brushed against them. They passed through fields of barley, now as brightly green as the luminous weed in the stream; through potato patches; through fields of beans and millet and pumpkins as full and red as the morning sun in winter. When at last they reached the maize fields they stopped.

Gradually other families arrived. Kalchu's two brothers, and their wives and children, worked the surrounding plots, their father's land having been split three ways among his sons. In the corner of one of their fields the younger brother's wife built a shelter of leaves and twigs draped across with a shawl and put her baby beneath it to shield her from the alternate onslaughts of sun and showers.

Later in the afternoon the wind rose and black storm-clouds rolled inexorably down the valley. When finally they opened, rain poured down in torrents, pelting the drooping maize fronds, pitting the bare earth where it landed. Chola and Mina crouched under home-made umbrellas – sheets of birch-bark bound in a mesh of split bamboo – that spread across their backs like the splayed wings of a moth. Kalchu, wearing only his loincloth, let the rain course over his bare skin. Gradually, as they worked, their feet sank into the soft earth and wet mud oozed up between their toes.

When the sun came out, steam rose and the air was too heavy to breathe. Chola lay down on the rug and fell asleep. Mina went to fetch some drinking water, taking the twins with her to bathe in the marshy pool around the spring. On the way back, she filled a pouch in the corner of her shawl with the edible weeds that grow like tongues of spinach among the crops.

Towards evening dark clouds gathered again over the mountain at the mouth of the valley, slashing its face with rain in a slanting sheet of steel-grey light. When the wind rose, cold with moisture, they began to pack up their things. Kalchu cut and stripped two stalks of maize for Hārkini and Lāla Bahādur and as they ambled along they chewed them like sugar-cane. When the sweetness was all sucked out they murmured that their legs were tired, and cried until they were picked up and carried home.

The first big globes of rain splattered their backs as they reached the village. When Kāli came back with the cows only minutes later, she was caught in the full force of the downpour. Rounding the bend from the top path down towards the stable she was brandishing a stick, beating the cows' dripping rumps and cursing them aloud for refusing to hurry.

Later, when the sheep came in, the rain had stopped. The air was breathlessly still, spent with raining, and coils of midges spiralled silently up and down.

Although it was still early morning the air was stale. No fresh cool wind had swept through the valley for days, and the same stagnant air had been breathed in and out a hundred times by the whole gasping village.

Chola was inside making *rotis*. In the added heat of the fire beads of sweat welled on her forehead, rolled down the furrows of her face and, gaining momentum, dropped weightily on to the ground. Flies zigzagged across the room, speeding about their business like bees in swarm. As Chola was kneading the dough, they hovered over it in hissing black droves, and she stopped occasionally to pick out the ones she accidentally squashed, like currants.

They ate outside but the flies, with dogged persistence, spoiled their food. Everyone had seen the dead dog on the path, bloated and grey and bald where it lay in the mud, and the heaps of excrement, all teeming with the same flies that were sharing their food; and the association flooded their throats like vomit.

Even the rain no longer seemed fresh; it congealed in the sullied air, splattering into filthy stinking puddles, hammering the roof and churning up the packed mud until it was slushy and loose. In the mornings Kalchu beat the mud down with a flat wooden spade to compress and seal it. But still the roof leaked, every day in a different place, a steady drip, drip of muddy water, like a clock ticking in the room below.

One evening the stars came out and the whole sky shone as clear as polished jet. It was as though the village had been underground and now, as it surfaced, the space was dazzling. Kalchu, Nara and Kāli slept outside under a rug. But towards morning heavy clouds spread across. Soaking wet, they moved inside and tried to sleep. But the heat and the endlessly pestering fleas and bedbugs dragged them, again and again, back to consciousness.

Up on Jimale, the south-facing mountain slope where every year the cultivated land is extended further into the surrounding forest, they were harvesting the wheat. When it had been cut and bound into sheaves, Kalchu carried it back to the village and laid it out on racks inside the house until it was dry enough to thresh. It took him two days, making three journeys a day – down the slippery path through the forest, then a mile along the river-bank, across the permanent bridge and up through the fields to the village.

After the harvest Kāli brought up the cows to graze the stubble and fertilize the fields for next year's buckwheat crop. At night the whole family slept in a rough shelter on the corner of their land and at the edge of the forest. They rebuilt it every year out of slats of wood and branches, with sheets of birch-bark for a roof.

When Chola got up in the morning the hut was like a dark capsule afloat in mist. She walked round and lifted one of the slats from the roof of the lean-to chicken coop. Five hens and a cockerel half-hopped, half-fluttered out. The cockerel stood braced, shrilling its cry out into the mist, answering other calls from other compounds up and down across the hillside. Chola stooped and felt around inside the coop for eggs. Then, making a soft purring sound she scattered a handful of maize kernels on to the ground in front of her and the hens stuck out their necks and stalked across.

Adjoining the other end of the hut was a small cattle-byre. Its three walls were built out of stones cleared from the surrounding cultivated fields. There was no roof and the rain that had fallen in the night left dark stripes where it trickled down the greasy surface of the cows' rumps.

Kalchu had brought in the two calves from their separate pen and they were pumping their mothers' udders, bracing their hooves and thrusting with the whole length of their sketchy bodies. He allowed them just enough milk to supplement the grass they were learning to eat and then pushed them aside, replacing their mouths on the teats with his fingers, squeezing the milk in short squirts into a frothing bowl on the ground below.

Later, inside the hut, the first rays of sun shone through the birch-bark roof, lighting it up like red cellophane and tinting the loose pine-needles on the floor the colour of ripe apricots. The cooking fire had been put out, but the smell of wood-smoke lingered, mixed with the cloying richness of fresh and sour milk and pine.

Kalchu, Chola and the children were eating, sitting in a circle around the empty hearth – a pit in the earth surrounded by stones. Behind them, stacked against the wall, were two folded blankets, some cooking pots, a sack of flour, another of potatoes, and a wooden jar where one day's surplus milk was set aside to curdle. There were no windows in the hut, but the open doorway looked out over the mountainside across the valley to the emerald paddy fields and, far away to the east, the village.

It was raining on Jimale, Chola and Mina had taken their claw-shaped wooden rakes and gone with a group of women to gather pine-needles in the forest. Kalchu's younger brother had come over from his neighbouring hut and the two men sat spinning, talking and looking after the small children until their wives returned. Kāli and three young friends hovered excitedly. They were going to spend the day in the forest, gathering mushrooms and wild strawberries.

Where they entered the forest, at the same level as their plots of land, the trees were mainly deciduous – walnuts, chestnuts and birches. It was sheltered inside, but they could hear the continuous swish of the rain in the branches high above them. Occasionally a heavy drop would fall through and land with a splat as hollow as the sound of condensation dripping in an empty cave.

They wandered on up the hillside. On the flatter stretches they talked and laughed; where the path rose more steeply they lapsed into silence, each lost in her own thoughts. Somewhere out of sight, cicadas filled the air with their high-pitched whirring and, in the distance, a woodpecker shrieked as it swooped from tree to tree in a flash of yellow, green and red.

The first strawberry patch was in a clearing where the under-growth was thick and leafy. As they began to gather the berries, eating the sweetest, darkest red ones, and putting the rest into their baskets to take home, the sun came out. For an instant its bright light glistened on a thousand shades of wet green leaves. Then the clouds came over and the colours faded.

The path that left the glade was steep and narrow and spread across with ivy and clumps of mauve and white violets. They'd passed beyond the deciduous woods, and the trees on either side were conifers – larch, spruce and pine.

Occasionally one or other of the girls left the path to go and pick a mushroom that she'd seen half-concealed behind a root or stone, or pushing through the surface of the pine-needles. At one point they came across a patch that was filled with every different kind of mushroom that they knew – white ones that grew like jagged clumps of coral, thick orange ones that oozed blue liquid when their stalks were broken, delicate saucer-shaped ones called *baṭuka*, meaning bowl.

When they left that patch their baskets were half-full, and the mushrooms, rubbing together and crushed, smelled of the forest, of dead wood and leaf-mould mixed with fresh wild herbs.

As they approached the top of the hill, the pine trees were taller and less dense. They could hear the rustle of the wind tossing the highest branches and see the bright light of the sky opening out beyond. The plateau stretched before them, an undulating sea of grassy dips and hollows. Some horses from the village, which were left to graze untended for the monsoon months, looked up as they passed. They walked on; the grass beneath their bare feet was smooth and wet and dotted with pink-and-white mountain flowers. A swallowtail butterfly sauntered past.

After a while they came across a herd of buffaloes. Beyond them was the Bārakotes' hut, made of wood and birch-bark like their own on Jimale. Every year the Bārakotes brought their buffaloes north, walking for ten days, because their own pastures were overgrazed and arid. Then, in winter, when this grass was deep in snow, the villagers here would take their sheep south to graze the Bārakotes' land.

They went into the hut and the Bārakotes gave them each a bowl of buffalo milk. They sat there for a long time, drinking their milk, gazing out at the grey drizzle while the Bārakotes told them stories about their home in the south, about the brightly coloured saris that the women wear, about the bazaars, and all the shops and stalls with beads and bangles, oranges, lemons, spices, chilli.

When they left, the rain had stopped and the clouds had cleared. Far away to the east a chain of jagged mountains jutted almost imperceptibly across the sky. Suddenly a cold wind rose from nowhere. They hurried across the plateau, afraid of being caught on the forest path after dark, glad that the wind was behind them,

billowing out their skirts and propelling them forward on legs
that ran involuntarily.

The village was almost deserted; only the old stayed behind –
some were too sick or weak or crippled to climb the path to Jimale.
Even the animals had gone – the cows and chickens to Jimale;
the horses wherever they chose to wander, where the wind blew
and the grass was thick; the sheep to their mountain grazing-
land to the north of the village, facing Jimale across the valley.
  Heavy doors were pulled across, their latches slotted into place.
Weeds and thistles sprouted freely on the roofs, growing tall and
strong, bursting into flower, then seed, triumphantly. The upper
path was deep in mud; the lower one was now a stream. Everywhere mud and water mixed with excrement and filth. Even the
drinking water, gushing through the bronze cow's head water
spout, was clouded up and grey with silt.

In any other season you could have looked down from a ridge
just below the pastures where the sheep were grazing and seen
the village in miniature, a dolls' farm set in a patchwork of
agricultural land that spread across the valley floor. And if your
eyes followed the river westwards, you could have looked up from
the valley directly on to the bald patch that was the cultivated
land midway up the forested slope of Jimale. But now in the
monsoon, Sigarup, Murti Lāl and the sheep inhabited a celestial
world of their own, a patch of grassland in a stratosphere of
densely swirling mist and cloud.
  Sometimes, when the clouds were stretched more thinly, the
confines of their world extended. The patch of grassland became
a narrow plateau. To the north and east, banks of scree rose
sheerly to the rocky crags and pinnacles surrounding the permanently snow-capped mountain peak, that in other seasons
loomed like a sentinel above the village.
  In the middle of the plateau was their shepherd's hut. A stream
meandered past it and cascaded into the depths of the forested

cliffside. Flowing straight across the rocks from the slowly melting snow, the water seemed as cold and as perfectly clear as glacial ice.

In the morning Sigarup went with the dog to graze the sheep. Leaving Murti Lāl at the hut to guard the lambs, he wandered off into the mist, whistling to the sheep as he steered them up across the bare rock face to a higher plateau, where the ground was marshy and the grass coarse and wiry and spiked with reeds. Later in the season he and Murti Lāl would come up here to gather rare medicinal herbs to take to sell in Aula in the autumn.

All day he wandered through the muffling silence of the clouds. Even the rain when it fell, fell silently; and the wind, when it came in occasional gusts, blew noiselessly over the treeless plateau. The only sounds to be heard were the sheep's teeth tearing grass and their low, rumbling bleats.

Once Sigarup thought he saw a *tār*, a flash of greyish-blue streaking away into the mist. It was here, in autumn and winter, that the men used to come and hunt the herds of *tār*. Usually, at this time of year, they stayed out of sight right up in the highest mountain peaks, where the monsoon rains fall as snow. Many years ago, one of the hunters had drowned in a shallow lake further out across the plateau. For a long time afterwards the shepherds said they heard his ghost at night, quietly sobbing.

In the evening, when Sigarup took the flock back to the hut, the lambs that had stayed behind bleated and frolicked with excitement. Murti Lāl held them back until Sigarup had milked the ewes. Then they let them suckle.

Later, when it was dark, they sat inside the hut beside a fire of thin bamboo, all there was to burn for firewood this high up above the treeline. When they had eaten their meal of wheat *roṭis* and milk they kept the fire going for a long time. Resting on three stones above the flames was a large copper pan full of milk, which Sigarup stirred from time to time as it was boiling. Eventually, when it had reduced enough he would let it cool to a sweet sticky paste, called *haut*.

When the fire was out the hut grew cold and the two boys settled down for the night under their blankets. Occasionally, they heard a pack of jackals howling, and the dog guarding the sheep outside would growl and bark a warning to them. Sometimes the dog would bark for no apparent reason and they assumed that it had sensed a wildcat or a leopard stealing up in silence through the darkness.

At the end of September it seemed as if the monsoon was drawing to a close. Often at dawn the sky would be perfectly clear and the air had the crispness that heralds the first night frost. In the afternoon clouds still swept through the valley, but the showers were lighter and less prolonged. People had moved back down from their temporary dwellings on Jimale and the village was once again alive with activity.

Then one morning, unexpectedly, the familiar, charged stillness of the early monsoon again hovered over the valley – enclosing it like a cocoon, with its own slow pulse-beat and heavy silent breathing. Later in the afternoon the first peals of thunder rolled across the sky. Gradually the sound came closer until it was bellowing overhead, hurling its echo from mountain to mountain over the valley.

With the first gusts of wind black clouds spread across the sky, growing slowly thicker until it was almost as dark as night. A buzzard soared overhead, its heavy wings braced so that it rose effortlessly, drifting with the air-stream.

Finally the rain came, slowly at first in single drops, then in a sudden burst that pelted the houses like shrapnel. All through the night it continued, and all through the night thunder boomed and lightning ripped across the sky in jagged white flashes.

It rained for four days. In the morning Kāli took the cattle out to graze, but after a couple of hours she came back soaked to the skin. Everyone else sat inside, biding time, watching muddy water drip, then trickle through the roof, watching the puddles spread across the floor where it landed.

Sometimes in the evenings Kalchu would sit outside under the eaves, scanning the horizon, willing the sky to change. He said he was worried about the crops, and he was worried about Sigarup still high in the mountains with the sheep. He talked about landslides in previous monsoons that had opened gaping chasms in the cliff behind the village. Sometimes, he said, he wondered if one year the cliff would topple completely, flattening the houses into a formless heap of rubble.

Then on the fifth day, mid-morning, a pool of light as pale and clear as moonstone appeared on the horizon. Suddenly the wind rose and, within seconds, the light had extended in a broad band across the sky. When the sun came out a rainbow formed and the air was so clear that each pine tree on the distant mountains, where usually the forest is a shadowy blur, stood out separate and distinct.

When the rain had stopped completely Kāli joined the flow of women making their way towards the stream to refill their water containers. Chola and Mina set out for the fields to continue the millet harvest, and Kalchu fetched the flat wooden spade and began beating down the mud to repair the leaking roof. Soon the whole valley was resounding with the same thud, thud, whack, from every rooftop in the village.

SĀUN SAṄKRĀNTI

EARLY IN THE MORNING, ON THE DAY BEFORE THE FESTIVAL OF *Sāun Saṅkrānti*, Mina and Kāli went with their baskets to collect some clay from the seam outside the village. Today they were going to replaster the house; not just the floor, which they did regularly when it became cracked and dusty, or on special occasions, such as when the house had been polluted by childbirth or death. Today they were going to replaster the whole house: floors, ceilings, walls – inside and out.

When they came back with their loads, Kalchu and Chola had cleared the house. The back of the roof was piled high with their possessions. There were two hand-hewn wooden chests, one filled with grain, the other with cloth; there were cooking pots of all sizes, with their bottoms blackened from the fire; there were shiny brass plates and bowls; there were iron cooking tripods, agricultural tools, winnowing fans, pestles, balls of wool and spindles, rugs, blankets, clothes; there was Kalchu's locked box where he kept money and bits of broken jewellery. Even the clusters of medicinal herbs, which were tied to the rafters to dry, had been brought outside and carefully stacked away.

Mina and Kāli dumped their loads and Kāli went down to the stable to fetch some cow-dung. Cow-dung is said to make the mixture more pliable; without it the plaster would crack as soon as it was dry. But cow-dung also purifies. Smoothed over the floor and walls, it wipes away pollution in the house.

Standing on opposite sides of the pile, Mina and Kāli beat it with wooden spades, softening the clay and mixing in the cow-dung. When it was ready they each fetched a huge bronze pan, the ones that were used for cooking rice at weddings, or boiling barley for making *raksi*. Into these they put a few handfuls of the clay and cow-dung mixture and then, adding water, kneaded it until it was liquid and as pale and frothing as freshly-churned cream.

While they were working outside on the roof, Chola was inside sweeping down the walls and ceiling, the beams and rafters. Torrents of debris were dislodged. In places the accumulated plaster of years, too heavy to bear its own weight, had cracked and crumbled, and fallen to the ground before her brush like broken china. Above the fireplace a layer of furry soot clung to the under-surface of the beams: on their upper surface flakes of chaff, from the autumn threshing on the roof, had lodged themselves in pockets, and as she swept, the black and yellow particles cascaded to the ground, then floated up on a cloud of swirling dust.

At last everything was ready. Mina and Kāli covered their hair with their oldest shawls and, struggling together, slopping the contents, they carried the heavy pans into the house.

The previous morning Kalchu had gone to the forest and gathered an armload of bamboo plants. At home in the afternoon he had bound them together in clusters to make three new brooms. For plastering they had to be fresh and supple with the green leaves still intact. Afterwards the plaster would be washed off and the brooms, now brittle twigs, would be used for months to come to sweep the floor.

Kāli and Mina swirled their brooms round the pan until they were saturated. Then they pulled them out and, drawing their arms right back from the shoulder, swished them forward through the air until they slapped against the wall. A fine spray of liquid mud and cow-dung showered across the room and, as the brooms hit the wall, ricocheted and settled on their clothes and faces.

Gradually the pale patches of fresh plaster spread across the blackened walls. Mina did the ceiling because Kāli was too small to reach. Stretching to her full height, she slapped the plaster on the sides and undersurface of the beams, and on the lengths of roof exposed between them. From time to time, as she looked up, specks of gritty plaster landed in her eyes and, putting her broom down for a moment, she dabbed them with the corner of her shawl.

Kāli refilled her pan with plaster and kneaded it to the right consistency. Then Chola helped her carry it through to the inner room where the family sleeps for warmth in winter. She was working in almost total darkness. There were no windows in the thick stone walls and the sunlight which brightened the outer room in a single shaft directed through the open doorway hardly penetrated the second inner room.

By the early afternoon the inside of the house was finished. Mina and Kāli were drenched. Their clothes and bare feet, their hands and faces, the wisps of hair that strayed from their shawls were stiff with slowly drying mud. Even their teeth and lips were speckled brown.

Chola went for a third time to fetch some water from the river while Mina and Kāli set to work on the outside of the house. A sprig of *dāṅtelo* had been fixed above the lintel to protect the house from evil, and Kāli left it in place, carefully plastering around it. Then she coated the thick planks of the door and moved along to work with Mina on the walls and eaves.

Gradually other women finished the insides of their houses and came outside to work in the sunlight. Right across the village muddy figures worked on every rooftop, thrashing walls with brooms in rhythmic sweeps, projecting showers of spray high and wide all around them.

When at last the work was finished, Mina and Kāli packed a basket with some clean clothes and went together to the stream to wash.

In the warmth of the afternoon sunshine they took off their jackets and, hitching up their skirts to their knees, waded out into the water. Torrents of mud poured from their bodies, flowed for an instant in a homogeneous brown cloud, and then dispersed, filtered by the current.

As the afternoon wore on, more and more women began to arrive. The river-bank echoed with their shouts and laughter and their splashing as they washed. Some were rinsing brooms; some were scrubbing clean the pans they'd used for plastering, scouring them with river silt and grass. Mina was squatting on the bridge, beating her muddy skirt with a piece of wood, then trailing the yards of material into the water so the loosened mud was washed away. Kāli was rinsing her hair, bent double under the brass cow's head water-spout out of which water, redirected from the river further up, gushed white and frothing.

When they'd finished washing Mina and Kāli draped their clean wet clothes among the hundreds of others stretched between the scraggy thorn trees. The river bank looked like the breeding ground of a flock of giant bats, their tattered wings extended and ruffled slightly by the wind.

They joined a group of women sitting talking on the bank. Someone lit a *chillim* and passed it round. One of the women was cleaning a necklace of silver rupees with an old toothbrush, scrubbing the coins one by one, then leaning over the bank to rinse them in the river till they shone. Mina began to comb Kāli's hair, carefully easing out the tangles, and squashing lice between her thumb-nails.

When the sun began to sink and the evening grew cold, they stripped their clothes from the thorn trees, collected together their pans and bamboo brooms and set out across the bridge for home.

The following day was *Sāun Sankranti*, the eve of the month of *Sāun* and the day of the festival.

As the first rays of morning sunlight streamed through the open doorway, the newly-plastered room looked as though it had been covered in the night by a fine layer of pinkish-buff snow. Everything was the same colour – floor, walls, ceiling, door, the three cylindrical grain containers in the corner. Every angle, line and contour were gently rounded as though the snow had drifted slightly in the wind.

At midday, Chola, Mina and Kāli came back from the fields to prepare the food for the evening. Mina and Kāli went to husk the rice at the stone mortar in the village square. Standing on opposite sides of the mortar, they pounded alternately to a rhythm Mina chanted as she lifted her arms up, then brought the pestle heavily down, so it landed, thud, in the centre of the pool of grain.

When they'd finished, Mina put the rice, a handful at a time, into the winnowing fan and tossed it into the air. The loosened husks floated away with the wind and the heavy whitish grains dropped straight back down.

As they were working, the smell of *puris* frying wafted over from the houses round the square.

At dusk Śaṅkar came back with the cows. He was carrying a bunch of ragwort that he'd picked while the cows were grazing on the Kālādika. He handed the flowers to Kāli, then drove the cows in through the stable door.

Kāli took the flowers up to the roof. At the top of the ladder she turned, and balanced a single flower on the uppermost notch. Then she moved about a yard to her right and laid another one at the edge of the roof with the yellow head pointing outwards. She went right round the edge of the roof, carefully distributing flowers as she went.

While she was working, Kalchu came up the ladder carrying a basket of *jharo*, the resinous wood that's gouged from deep inside the trunks of the oldest, tallest pine trees, then cut into chips and burned for lighting. He arranged the *jharo* in two pyramids at the edge of the roof, between the flowers.

Slowly dusk began to settle into darkness. From the height of the rooftop they could see right over to the Kālādika, where one patch of sunset still remained, splashed across the sky, like a spilled pot of paint. To each other on the roof, they were shadows moving round, bending down. Only the flowers stood out brightly, as though in the half-light they were very slightly luminous.

Much later – at the time of night that belongs to owls and jackals, when human beings are strangers – Kalchu left the house and climbed the hill behind the village. At the top as he walked across the plateau, he could see the light from the fire in the main shrine, flickering through the open door and out between the pillars of the veranda. Already there were people there, silhouettes that wandered back and forwards in the firelight.

Kalchu took off his shoes and went into the shrine. Inside he lit a piece of *jharo* from the fire. Then, carefully shielding the flame with his cupped hand, he carried it back to the village.

All the way from the shrine down the hillside and through the pine trees, hundreds of flames glowed like the roving eyes of night-prowling animals. Only when they came close was it possible to make out the dark shadow of a hand and arm carrying each one, the sketchy outline of a black body behind, and above, a ghoulish half-lit face with gaping shadowy craters for mouth and eyes.

Kalchu climbed on to the roof of the house, and with the flame he'd brought from the shrine fire set light to the two piles of *jharo*.

Soon afterwards fires were blazing on every rooftop in the village, and in every shrine all around its outskirts to the north, the south, the east and the west; in the fields, at the crossroads, by the river, in the forest.

The whole family was outside now. The twins and Nara were chasing each other round and round, hiding in the shadows, then bursting out on each other, screaming, wild with uncontrolled excitement.

Sigarup picked up a piece of unlit *jharo* and held it in the fire until it was blazing and drips of flaming resin fell from it, spluttering to the ground. Then he hurled it off the roof as far as he could, shouting at the top of his voice a threat to all evil spirits; warning them that tonight was the night they must leave the village for good. The *jharo* flared through the darkness, twisting and somersaulting, spiralling down until it landed in the village square, flickered momentarily, then died.

Kāli lit another piece of *jharo*. As she bent down over the fire, her nose-ring and the silver coins of her necklace glinted fiercely. Then, standing up and leaning back into the shadow, she flung the *jharo* with all the strength she possessed across the border of flowers and into the dark pool of space beyond the firelit roof. 'Get out of our village and don't ever come back.'

On other rooftops black figures moved back and forth between firelight and shadows. Missiles blazed in every direction through the darkness, crossing paths in zigzags. Some soared up and down in gentle arcs; some shot horizontally; some rocketed high into the sky, then turned about and suddenly plummeted.

Women's voices, men's voices, children's voices screeched out curses and threats. Individually, each one would have been lost, swallowed immediately into the immense space of the night. But together they surged like a tide across the valley, seeking out witches, ghosts and demons; purging their haunts behind rocks, in the highest swaying branches of the pine trees, in the whirlpools by the burning *ghaṭ* where the two great rivers meet.

At one end of the village a gun was fired. Before its echo died another sounded, and another, followed in quick succession by two more from the opposite side of the village. Dogs began to bark, triggering a rallying cry, a droning chorus broken occasionally by one or other's high-pitched howling. Then, from somewhere, the sound of kettledrums rolled out. Another set pitched in from the north of the village, another from the south. Their rumbling vibrations set the whole valley quaking.

Far in the distance the fires of Pere village shimmered like the electric lights of a city. And on the other side of the river, Gorigāuṅ, hidden from sight by the curve of a wooded hillside, projected above itself a pale orb of hazy reddish light.

Kalchu came up the ladder carrying a cockerel. In the firelight its comb and the loose folds of flesh at its throat glowed like broken mirrors reflecting the embers of the fire. The feathers of its tail, shiny strips of shot-silk in blue, black, green and russet, drooped down over the dark folds of Kalchu's sleeve. Its eye, a tiny pinprick, gazed unblinking into the darkness.

Kalchu put it down on the roof and clamped the body between his knees. Then, stretching out its neck with his left hand, he sawed off the head. Dark blood welled up and spread, like a slick of oil, across the feathers.

Kalchu held a bowl of rice grains to catch some drops of blood. Then he released the headless cockerel. The body

103

convulsed, flopping around the roof in a series of uncoordinated half-somersaults, leaving a trail of blood like footprints.

Kalchu stood up, holding the bowl of rice and blood, and threw a few grains into the air in four directions. 'Before you go, we offer you the life of this bird. We bear you no malice and hope that when you leave our valley your journey is a good one. But we ask you now, Spirits of the Night, never to return.' He muttered the incantation so it was barely audible. Then he went up to every member of the family, beginning with Chola and ending with the twins, marking blood-red *ṭikās* between their eyes.

The fire was dying. The twins stood over it, stirring the last embers with their feet. For a moment bright flames danced out of the charcoal, then there was darkness.

Downstairs, inside the house, Kalchu was preparing the cockerel by plunging it into a pan of boiling water, then plucking out its feathers by the handful. When it was as pale and bald as a fledgeling, he dismembered the body, hacked up the meat with a small adze and dropped the cut pieces into a pan of hot oil.

While the meat was simmering, they ate *puris* and spiced potatoes. Kalchu's two brothers came in and they too were given *puris* and bowls of *raksi*. *Chillims* of tobacco were lit and passed around. Then, when the rice and meat were ready, Mina fetched some pots of river-water from the big copper container in the corner and everyone washed their hands where they were sitting round the fire. Chola sprinkled a few grains of rice from the top of the pan into the fire for the gods and began to serve the food.

When everyone else had finished eating, Chola filled her own plate with the remains of the meat and rice. Mina piled up the plates and took them outside to wash, and the dog rummaged round the floor in search of bones.

After the fourth and last bottle of *raksi* had been drunk, Śaṅkar got out the double-ended drum brought back from India by his grandfather many years ago. After a few false starts he found his rhythm and everyone began to clap in time. Then Kalchu, the only one who knew the words to the Indian song, started singing. A moment later, amid great surges of laughter, Kāli wound her mother's necklace of silver coins three times round her slender ankle, pulled her young cousin to her feet, and together the two of them began to dance.

It was Indian dancing; poised and erotic, unlike the sombre local dances. Only children ever danced like this, and when Kāli was older and married she'd probably be ashamed to admit she even knew the movements.

Very slowly, she began to roll her hips, young girl's hips without a trace of roundness. Her hands were held out to the sides, circling supplely, fingers gesturing elegantly. Her bare foot stamped the ground and the necklace clattered. Once, for an instant, she lost her concentration and a smile cracked across her features. Then the Indian dancer's mask was back: head held up defiantly, lips pouting, eyes seductive yet reproving.

As soon as the song finished she grabbed her cousin and the two of them sank into a heap on the floor, hiding their faces and giggling. Everyone else was laughing too. A crowd of people who'd heard the music and the laughter from outside stood in the doorway, smiling bemusedly. Then they came in and joined the others sitting round the fire.

Not long afterwards, when the visitors had left, Chola fetched the rugs from the inner room and the family lay down around the fire and slept.

Dawn came, a thin band of light as clear and colourless as water. Kāli was the first up. Still half-asleep, she began collecting the flowers she'd arranged the night before. The roof was littered with charcoal, debris from the fire; the flowers, scrunched and trampled under many feet, were pale and wilted. When she'd been right round the edges of the roof and gathered all the flowers into a bunch, she climbed down the ladder and began to walk along the back path out of the village.

The air was very still and drops of dew were poised in perfect globes on blades of grass and leaves. A new crop of irises had opened since the day before and the long grass on the river-bank was flushed with blue and purple.

Kāli crossed the small bridge and followed the path until it split in two, one continuing west towards the Bazaar, the other heading north across the Kālādika towards Chaura and Chhuma. At the point of the crossroads there was a heap of dead flowers. Kāli threw down her bunch of ragwort and it landed, splayed out limply, on the top.

On her way back she stopped to wash her hands and face in the cold water. When she was almost home she picked a sprig of *dāṅtelo*, pricking her thumb on a thorn and sucking the blood that rose to the surface. At the doorway she reached up and slotted the new *dāṅtelo* twig between the stones above the lintel. Then she pulled the old one out and threw it away, over the edge of the roof.

PART II

THE *KARASO*

ONE AFTERNOON KĀLI BROUGHT THE COWS HOME EARLY AND CAME
rushing over to ask me to go to the forest with her to collect a
load of pine-needles. Her mother had told her to bring back at
least one load before it got dark, and it would be much more fun
if I went with her. I'd seen Chola and Mina setting out for the
forest in the early morning, and three times during the day I'd
watched them coming back, stooped over and staggering under
the weight of the enormous loads that spread across their backs,
stretching three times broader than their shoulders and several
feet above their heads. Each time I'd wondered how they carried
such a heavy load; how the pine-needles even stuck together,
bound as they were with a single length of rope. 'All right,' I said.
'But I'm not sure how much use I'm going to be.'

Kāli was delighted. Smiling broadly to herself she closed the
heavy wooden door behind us and fastened the little chain latch
on to a nail on the adjacent door. Then, standing on tiptoe, she
reached up into the eaves where the agricultural tools were stored,
and pulled out two wooden rakes, *karasos*, and two lengths of
hemp-fibre rope. She carefully wound one of the lengths of rope
round and round, from hand to elbow to form a coil, then tied it
in the middle so that two loops, like the loops of a bow, protruded.
Into one of these she fixed the *karaso*. The other she draped across
her forehead, so the *karaso* dangled down her back. She smiled as
I watched and copied her, carrying my tools the local way.

We climbed down the notched-pole ladder and picked our way
through the muddy ground towards the back path, passing the
neatly stacked woodpile and the growing heap of freshly gathered
pine-needles.

'It gets bigger every time you look,' said Kāli proudly. 'Yesterday
it was only up to my knees; by tomorrow or the next day it'll be
this high at least.' Grinning conspiratorially, she reached up

as high as she could, contorting her small body but not quite jumping.

The season for gathering pine-needles had begun five days ago. There'd been a ceremony called *ban pasāi*, the entering of the forest. All the women in the village had dressed in their best clothes with their hair freshly oiled and plaited, their earrings, nose-rings and necklaces of Indian silver rupees washed and glinting in the sunlight. Together they'd made their way to a place on the opposite side of the river, where the forest dropped right down, meeting the bank. Here some of the younger women had thrown down their tools and gathered in a big circle, singing and dancing, while older women and children watched from the sidelines, shouting encouragement. Then, as suddenly as lightning streaks through the sky, they'd disbanded, scrabbled for their ropes and *karasos* and disappeared, shrieking, into the forest.

When I'd asked Chola what the ceremony was for she'd said she didn't know: they'd always done it. But in times gone by, there'd been a feast at *ban pasāi*; the women had brought rice and huge copper pans to the forest. There they'd lit a fire and cooked the rice, but before starting to eat they'd made an offering to Ban Bhāi, god of the forest, asking permission to plunder his lands. In those days too, there'd been another festival a month or so later, called *ban chhorāi*, the leaving of the forest. After that, even if your pile at home was only ankle-deep, no one was allowed to take a single load of pine-needles out of the forest.

'Last year,' said Kāli, as we walked along behind the houses, 'Mother and one or two other women started before the forest was officially opened – before *ban pasāi* – and people were so angry that they made the women's husbands go to the headman and pay a fine of five rupees each.'

'Why was that?' I asked, wondering if they'd been angry on behalf of Ban Bhāi because Chola and the other women hadn't waited for his permission, or because they'd cheated, sneaking out first and grabbing all the pine-needles at the edge of the forest without having to climb at all.

'I don't know,' said Kāli; it was possible that the festival of *ban pasāi* had lost its association with the god of the forest before she was even born. 'But Father and the other men had a great time at the headman's – getting blind drunk on the *raksi* that they bought with the proceeds.'

Kāli chose the steeper, shorter route to the forest and we climbed at a leisurely pace, stopping occasionally to catch our breath, lurching drunkenly and bumping into each other when the gradient increased and we were too lazy to keep up our momentum.

There'd been a frost in the night, but now in the mid-afternoon the sun on our backs was strong and warm. The leaves on the thorn trees were almost open, and when we turned to look back at the distance we'd climbed, there were clusters of vivid green that trailed down the hillside and encompassed the village like waterweed.

There was a time when this entire hillside had been covered in forest but, being closest to home, the trees had been felled one after another for building and firewood. Now the bare earth was pitted and ravaged and, during the monsoon rains, torrents of water swept down the loosened topsoil, carving out gullies and chasms that crumpled occasionally into landslides.

It felt, as we struggled up the last, steepest stage of the hillside, that we were swimming in the white light of the sun. Slowly we made our way through the heat and the glare and arrived, at last, in the soothing shade of the trees. Kāli sat down on a flat stone, sighing with relief. In a moment or two, when she'd recovered, she produced her *chillim* and the little pouch of tobacco that she kept in her waistband. During the time that it took to prepare, I stretched out on my back, staring into the trees, listening to the wind teasing their branches.

'Have you got a light?' Kāli's voice brought me back to earth. She'd obviously been counting on me having one, because the *chillim* was poised at her lips, ready for her to pull in deeply when the surface leaves caught fire.

'No,' I said, and dejected but resigned, she took it from her mouth. We were about to carry on when we saw two women with their loads of pine-needles coming down the path towards us. As they approached and noticed the unlit *chillim*, one of them passed us her tinder, commenting with a smile that they'd got here just in time for all of us: they needed a smoke, and we needed a light. While Kāli fumbled, striking the flint against the steel, trying to produce a spark that was strong enough to light the little piece of cotton, they told me how pleased they were to see me working just like them. We smoked the *chillim* together and continued on our separate ways. After a while, I turned to watch them as they receded down the hillside – two lumbering animals, with bodies grossly disproportionate to their slender stick-like ankles.

Although the outskirts of the forest were carpeted with pine-needles, Kāli led me higher and deeper into the trees. Occasionally, as we walked, sunshine seeped through the canopy of branches, bathing the forest in clear pools of light, and women raking in the distance would be suddenly spotlit, their pine-needles turning from tawny to amber.

'This'll do,' said Kāli at last, and we stopped in a glade that was dominated by three great larches. I dropped my rope at the base of one of the trees and started to rake, struggling to keep from slipping on the steep slope with its loose pine-needle surface. Kāli stood over me for a while, watching critically. 'That's fine,' she said approvingly, and wandered off to begin her own pile twenty yards or so away.

The scent of the pine rose instantly, warm, fresh and powerfully evocative. In some places the needles were several inches deep and easier to rake than autumn leaves on a tended lawn; elsewhere they were saturated and packed, or buried among tangled creepers and virulent, shining ivy.

Once when I looked up Kāli was nowhere in sight. I wondered if she'd moved on to another place in the forest without saying anything, but when I stood perfectly still, I could hear the rhythmic scratching of her *karaso* from behind some trees, and the occasional tearing sound when she accidentally caught it in the undergrowth. Sometimes too, I could hear the distant sounds of other women, coughing or calling out to one another, laughing. Their voices sounded shrill and incongruous, violating the silence that was appropriate in the great dome of the forest.

My pile was growing. I wondered how big the pile at home would have to be to last the year. Every evening Kāli spread a new layer of pine-needles in the stable as bedding for the cattle. I'd often watched her carrying them from the pile outside, spreading them out, fluffing them up. At night the stable was always warm and dry, smelling of pine and the grassy breath of animals; in the mornings it was damp and ammoniac.

The stable was mucked out properly only once a year, in winter. Sometimes fresh cow-dung would be collected for plastering the house, for rituals, or for sealing the clay fermentation jars. Otherwise the shit and piss were left and, day after day, the soiled bedding was trampled down and compressed. After a year it was so hard that Chola and Mina had to hack it out with adzes. Last year it took them three full days to clear the stable and make a heap of the black peat-like *mal* outside. During that time the stench around the house was terrible.

Then, every morning before the sun was up, Chola and Mina would take the *mal* in basketloads and spread it on the paddy fields as fertilizer. Clouds of steam would rise as they scooped beneath the surface of the warm fermenting heap, and as they carried their loaded baskets through the frosty morning air.

In the springtime, after the irrigation channels had been opened and the paddy fields flooded, Kalchu would plough the *mal* into the soft wet earth, ready for the rice to be transplanted. In the course of many years the accumulation of *mal* had made the soil in the paddy fields so dark and rich that it was used as a black dye, together with the red and green dyes from wild plants and flowers, for printing skirts.

'Are you ready yet?' Kāli had come over and was eyeing my

rakings, stacked against a tree on the upper side of the incline to stop them slipping down.

'What do you think – is that enough?' I asked, unsure how much my inexperience showed.

'It looks pretty good to me,' she said. 'I'll show you how to bale and tie it up.'

She fetched my rope and laid it out on a clear patch of ground. Then, with great bravado, she attacked the pile of pine-needles, scooping them up between the giant clutch of her *karaso* and her own small hand, depositing them in another heap that she was building on top of the rope. When the entire pile had been transferred, she bunched the needles together with her hands and alternately stroked and beat them with her *karaso*, knitting them into a kind of rudimentary bale.

When she'd retrieved the ends of the rope and tied it all together, she sat with her back against the load, adjusting the carrying rope over her forehead. I stood behind her and, when she said the word, helped her to heave the load from the ground. Staggering slightly, she eventually lurched to her feet. Although she was gripping the rope at her shoulders, easing the weight on her head, her neck was fixed and immobile; to look at me she had to turn her entire body and raise her eyes in their sockets.

'How does it feel?' I asked.

'It's fine,' she said, but as soon as she took a few practice steps forward, the edges of the bale, on either side of the binding rope, started to sag and collapse. It wasn't long before a steady stream of pine-needles was flowing down behind her like water from a leaking *gāgro*.

Disconcerted, she admitted that she'd only done this once before, that, in all honesty, I could probably do it equally well on my own.

So she untied her disintegrating load and we started again, Kāli working on her own pile this time, I on mine. But, try as I might, I just couldn't grasp the principle. I couldn't understand how I could possibly make the individual pine-needles knit; it was like trying to carry grain in a net, or water in a cloth. Biting back feelings of inadequacy, frustration and anger I tied up the bundle as well as I could, resigning myself to losing most of it on the way down the hill, preparing for laughter and jeers when we got to the village.

Eventually we were ready to go and Kāli's load – for all her child's body – was considerably bigger than mine. But as we made our way down through the trees, I realized that even if I'd been better at baling I could never have carried that load: my forehead hurt, my neck felt stiff and strained, and the pine-needles on the path, compressed and polished by thousands of feet, were as slippery as glass.

Even Kāli had become quiet and subdued. Listening to her heavy breathing and her occasional vigorous sniffs, I could feel her concentration as she followed behind me as surely as a blind bat senses light.

Suddenly she stopped in her tracks, noticing something. 'Where's your *karaso?*'

'I wedged it into the pine-needles, as you did with yours. It must be there somewhere.' So she caught me up and turned me round, feeling my load from top to bottom and every side. But it wasn't there.

I couldn't believe it at first; I'd been so careful. An overwhelming feeling of inadequacy flushed through me again. Not only was I unable to help with the work, I couldn't even care for the family's tools. 'I'll go back and find it,' I said. Kāli insisted on coming with me, kind and concerned, but I persuaded her, in the end, to carry on home.

'Don't get lost,' she called after me as we went our separate ways.

Without Kāli, the path seemed narrower, less clearly defined, and there were little forks and side-tracks that I only half-remembered. But I followed landmarks – the glade of birch saplings; the drift of unmelted snow where Kāli had helped herself to a frozen drink; the huge pine tree whose trunk had been gouged to a tenth of its width for *jharo*. Kāli had told me that it was no longer used, that if one more chip were taken the entire tree would topple. The inner flesh was as raw as a recent wound, and clear resin had oozed to the surface, trickled down and set into sticky pink runnels.

Last autumn, at the full-moon festival in Gorigāuṅ, a *jharo* tree like that had fallen. The *dhāmis*, possessed by their gods, had been dancing in a clearing above the village. The drums had been too loud to hear the preliminary ripping, so when the tree suddenly crashed to the ground, no one moved. Everyone just stood there, astonished. The tree was so big that, if it had fallen into the clearing, it would have flattened most of the gathering, but luckily it went in the other direction, toppling over the cliffside.

For long stretches I walked with my eyes on the ground, mesmerized by the silence of the forest, by my own soundless footsteps.

The *karaso* was exactly the colour of pine-needles. Thinking about it now, for the first time, I realized that I'd no idea how a *karaso* was made: an arm-length shaft of wood, smooth and shiny as a newly opened conker, with five prongs at the end that were perfectly shaped into the smooth curves of a grasping hand. There were no special woodworking tools in the village – no saws or chisels or planes. Doors, wooden grain chests, roofing beams were merely hacked into shape with adzes. And it occurred to me that I neither knew how many the family owned nor how difficult mine would be to replace.

Sunlight penetrated the forest in long horizontal shafts. There was no one else in sight. I paused for a moment, unsure of which path to take. At some point Kāli and I had stopped climbing and branched off to the left; but this was too narrow, an animal track. It was difficult, too, to tell how far I'd come on my own; before, we'd been talking and time had probably passed quickly. But I recognized nothing. Sometimes the layout of trees seemed familiar, or the way a particular branch overshadowed the path. But then all the different images of trees that I'd seen – textures of bark, shades of green, angles at which the branches protruded – merged in my mind into one.

I realized I was lost when the sky suddenly lightened and I came out into a broad clearing. It was the monsoon settlement of some other village – five or six huts and a small area of once-ploughed land, enclosed by a tumbledown stone wall. Either the settlement was abandoned now, or the huts had been allowed to deteriorate during the winter. Loosened birch-bark flapped from the roofs and sections of the wooden walls lay sprawled on the ground, flattened by gales.

I slumped to the ground, despair weighing as heavily as the load on my back. At first I'd thought that Kāli was joking, that she'd sneaked up behind me, snatched the *karaso* and hidden it up her skirt or behind a tree. She loved to play like that, but she'd have told me in the end, exploding with laughter at my angry duped expression. Then I'd wondered if some women who'd stopped me on the path had taken it. But why would they – because they needed another *karaso*? as a practical joke against the foreigner?

A cold wind swept through the clearing and a few pinkish clouds passed out of sight. The sky became as clear and grey as a mountain rock-pool. Suddenly I felt totally alone. I didn't want to return to the village; I wanted to stay here in one of the huts and not see any of them ever again. But, after a moment or two, the childishness passed. I hoisted my load from the ground and lurched to my feet.

It was much darker under the trees now and, afraid of not reaching the village before nightfall, I branched off on to what I thought was a short-cut. But the path became narrower, more overgrown, and eventually petered out altogether, choked up with bracken and creepers and snarls of wild raspberry plants.

Retracing my steps, I realized with a shock that I was no more able to find my way back to the village than I'd been able to find the place we'd been raking. I had thought that, if the worst came to the worst, I could always follow the hillside and make my way down to the bottom. But the forest proved me wrong – I'd underestimated its intricacies.

I was about to take off my load and leave the heap of pine-needles for someone else to find in the morning when I saw a figure approaching in the distance. It was a long time before I could believe that it was really Kāli, come back to find me.

'We were worried,' she said. 'We thought you must have got lost.'

'I did get lost.'

She offered to carry my load, but I wouldn't let her. I just wanted her to take me back, to talk to me as she always did.

'Did you find the *karaso?*'

'I couldn't even find the place we were raking.'

'Never mind,' she said kindly, 'maybe someone else will pick it up and bring it back.'

She talked almost all the way down through the forest; and then, when we were out in the open she started again, 'Do you see those trees over there?' She was pointing at four or five pine-trunks sprawled at awkward angles over the hillside. 'That's the easiest way of getting your firewood – cut the trees at the edge of the forest and send them rolling down to the bottom. But you have to leave the wood to dry for a year before you take it home. If the forester finds green wood in your woodpile, you're in serious trouble. This way he knows live trees are being felled, but he doesn't know who's felling them.'

The forester had passed through the village recently. He was a city man, wearing a desert island shirt and a visor-cap that said Top Dog Disco in bold red lettering. The headman had killed a chicken for him and someone else had contributed a bottle or two of *raksi*.

'The trouble with foresters,' said Kāli, 'is that they're permanently hungry; feed them well and they'll leave you alone; forget to and they'll scour the entire village for evidence of green wood, musk, *tār* and all the other protected animals that you're not supposed to kill. They're like dogs – every bit as greedy.

'And you know the two foresters who live here in the village; they're fine when they're at home, but when they go to the village they're responsible for, in Dolpo, I bet they carry on like all the others do, terrorizing people.

'Last year' – she smiled mischievously – 'something really awful happened to one of them. They'd both been working for nearly two years, and all that time they hadn't been paid a penny. Then, one day, their government wages arrived – all at once, thousands of rupees. So that night they celebrated, getting roaring drunk, playing cards and gambling. One of them staked everything he'd got, and lost. Can you imagine' – she was giggling now – 'all that money in your pocket one minute, and the next minute – nothing.'

The path through the village, flanked on one side by the backs of the houses and on the other by the looming cliffside, was as pervasively dark as a cave and we kept stumbling over rocks, getting our feet wet in puddles and pools of mud.

Eventually we came out in the comparative brightness of the open space behind the house. I sank to the ground at the base of the heap of pine-needles, relieved that there was no one around to witness my exhaustion and the miserable size of my load. When I'd extracted my head from the carrying rope, Kāli un-tied the bale and started scooping up armloads of pine-needles and throwing them to the top of the pile. 'I told you,' she said, standing back when she'd finished. 'Look how it's grown, just today.'

Inside the house the fire was burning and a couple of sticks of *jharo*, resting one on top of the other on the stone hearth, cast a stark and ambiguous light. Everyone was eating. As we walked in through the door Kalchu looked up from his food and said in a worried voice, 'Where's your *karaso*, sister?' I was about to explain when I realized that Kāli had told him already. He started to smile, teasing me, and for the second time I was convinced that someone would flourish it back to existence, that it was all only a game.

*

121

'How do you make a karaso?' said Kalchu, repeating the question I'd just asked him. 'Well, first of all you have to find the right branch – a pine-branch that splays at the end into three, four or five separate limbs. Then you strip it of its bark and, while the wood is still green and supple, you bend back the thin limbs and bind them in place with string. When you've done that you have to leave it on a drying rack above the fire for . . . oh, I suppose about three months. Afterwards, when you take off the string, the soft fingers at the end of the arm have hardened into claws.'

'And how does it get to be so smooth and shiny?'

'That comes with years and years of raking: grass and pine-needles, grass and pine-needles.'

THE RED BITCH

WHEN THE RED BITCH CAME ON HEAT SHE WAS NEVER ALONE. Dogs followed her everywhere, watching, waiting, sniffing and from time to time mounting her. Sometimes she'd yelp and try to run away with her back hunched and her bushy tail sweeping the ground between her legs. Sometimes she'd turn on her heel, snarling, and lunge at a dog that had gradually edged over and positioned itself expectantly behind her. But most of the time she ignored the dogs that hovered around her as she slept in the sun or beavered around the village in pursuit of this or that scent. Her patience did wear thin but, in general, she resigned herself graciously to being the leader of the pack.

One evening the commotion in the village square was louder than usual. It wasn't just the sustained rumbling growls rising to a frenzy as two dogs threatened each other then lunged together in a bitter embrace, each asserting its place in the hierarchy, the priority of its rights over the red bitch. This was different; these were the sounds of distress – short staccato yelps broken by prolonged baleful howling.

I went out on to the roof to have a look and at first I could see nothing amiss. The dogs were there as usual, loitering in their pack. But then I noticed a group of children on the other side of the square, pointing and laughing. A stone hurtled through the air and the dogs scattered. In their midst was the red bitch, standing rump-to-rump with the *ḍāṅgri*'s black-and-tan mastiff mongrel. The stone hit her square on the flank and she yelped, but their genitals were so tightly locked together that neither dog could move.

The puppies were born by the woodpile and the red bitch strutted around proudly, her feathery tail waving high in the air behind her. Nara and the twins were endlessly fascinated with the little, blind, half-bald creatures, and spent hours picking them up and playing with them. Once they took one away from the woodpile and hid it in the stable and the mother searched everywhere, growing more and more distressed. But they were unable to spin out their game for long; impatience got the better of them and they returned the puppy, which stood shivering under its mother's tongue as she licked it clean of foreign influences. Not long afterwards the red bitch was sprawled on her side, asleep, with all six puppies climbing on top of each other, scrabbling for access to her swollen teats.

The red bitch was the seventh in a line of dogs that had belonged to Kalchu's family since his grandfather had brought the first one back from Tibet some forty years previously. That one had been big and powerful, a trained hunter, providing the family regularly with musk, *tār* and wild boar meat. But as the generations ran their course, each one interbreeding with the local village dogs, the successive progeny became smaller and relentlessly unimpressive. If hunting had once been in the red bitch's blood it had long since been bred out and forgotten. Her only real skill was her ferocity as a guard dog, watching over the sheep in the temporary grazing settlements high in the mountains or alerting the family to strangers within the village and intruders in the house. But even in this, the red bitch was not to be counted on; fierceness and docility alternated as unpredictably as the direction of the winds that flounced through the valley in the early monsoon.

Out of every litter the puppy that was always kept was the biggest, reddest female. One evening Kalchu went to the woodpile to choose which one it would be. Four of them were female, two male; all were varying shades of russet or tawny, but only one was the deep red that he liked. Squatting down, he picked up the other five squirming bodies and stuffed them into a cloth sack. When he set off towards the river the red bitch followed. He shouted at her and kicked out and she stopped in her tracks, yelping, but soon afterwards she caught him up again. Finally he picked up a handful of stones and every time he looked round and found her following, he threw one. Some hit her, some missed. Eventually she stopped, and sat motionless for a long time, watching him go. Then she turned and went back to her one remaining puppy.

The following morning when the twins found out what Kalchu had done they were angry and upset. But the red bitch chose that same day to pick up the remaining puppy in her teeth and carry it by the scruff of the neck up the ladder and into the house. The twins became preoccupied with the little round body, its eyes now open, as it trotted round the house playfully biting its mother's heels.

But in time the novelty wore off. The red bitch became short-tempered, snapping at the puppy when it went to suckle her dangling teats, now empty of milk; pushing it aside when it clambered over her sleeping body or pummelled her head in a rowdy mock fight. Chola too complained that there were now two dogs to get in the way and whinge for food. She shouted at them twice as often and the dogs in response yelped twice as loudly.

Everyone in the village had a healthy respect for the dogs' fierce-ness; attacks and injuries were commonplace. Usually it was safe to wander round the village in the daytime; the dogs knew their own people and, as long as neighbours stayed on neutral ground, they let them be. But before climbing the notched-pole ladder to another person's house, it was best to shout up from the ground, because the household dog was often waiting at the top, snarling viciously and waiting to attack. Most people, when they went out at night or approached another village, carried a stick or a handful of stones; if one or two dogs in a pack had been wounded the others would pick up the aggressive intention and drop back sullenly.

But more than fear I felt disgust; almost all of the dogs were painfully thin and many were diseased. One had mange so badly it was nearly bald; it moped around, scratching the exposed pink skin that had cracked and flaked where it stretched brittly over the jutting spine and ribcage. Others had festering wounds that seemed never to heal, or had adapted themselves to a three-legged gait, running as fast as the other dogs but with one leg, withered or deformed from birth, tucked up under their bodies. It was revolting to see these half-starved creatures snuffling around behind the houses or along the river-bank in search of excrement. I'd often come across one or other of the twins, squatting down outside the house, with the red bitch hovering by, waiting to eat the faeces. And when the twins were babies and shat in Chola's lap, she'd call out, 'Chu chu chu,' and the red bitch would come running in to clean the mess.

One summer, just before the monsoon, a team of government health workers came to the area to teach people about pre-ventative health care and sanitation. Sigarup was chosen as one of the village representatives and was paid twenty rupees for each of the five days that he attended the course. The sessions were held in the schoolroom and three nurses, in rippling saris, stood at the front of the room and demonstrated, with the use of pictures and a dummy, how intestinal worms and diseases are spread by eggs and germs that pass from one person's faeces to another person's mouth.

On the fifth and final day theory was put into practice and pits were dug for latrines. But after the health workers returned to Kathmandu little changed. The latrines were proclaimed dis-gusting and abandoned for the privacy of open spaces, and the red bitch continued to lick out the dirty dishes before Mina swilled them cursorily with river water.

But for all her dirty habits the red bitch was part of the family and I liked her; we all did. Too often she became a scapegoat for anger not strictly her due. When Chola was kneading the dough for *rotis*, tired after a day's work in the fields, exasperated by the twins' hungry grizzling, the chickens flapping around the bowl and the dogs' beady eyes, she'd lash out, screaming, and the red bitch would yelp exaggeratedly and skulk off to a corner. But when the puppy fell from the roof and broke its leg, Kalchu bound it to a splint with wool, replacing the bandage each time it slackened, until the bone had set. And sometimes, when there were visitors and *raksi* to drink, he'd get the red bitch to sing – a mournful, wailing dirge that made us fall about with laughter.

On winter nights the dogs would sleep inside, curled up by the remains of the fire or with the children under one of the goat's-hair rugs. Sometimes they'd wake in the night, alerted by the jackals howling on the outskirts of the village, and they'd nose open the heavy doors and go outside on to the roof, joining the other dogs in their chorus of barking. Eventually, when the howling had subsided and the jackals had sloped off to the forest, the dogs would come back in, or they'd wander off into the frosty night and not return until morning.

One day, when Chola was releasing the hens from the coop, she noticed that the cockerel was missing. The coop was on the roof, a few feet from the door to the house, and was a hollowed-out tree-trunk with a wooden slat for sealing the entrance at night. Jackals and martens could hardly have lifted the latch and, even if they had found their way in, there would have been signs of a scuffle: dead chickens, scattered feathers. The thief was human. Chola was furious. She went to the edge of the roof and shouted across the village at the unnamed thief that for this he'd be struck with paralysis; that he'd be smitten with cholera and die; that unless he owned up and returned the cockerel, the gods would punish his family with poverty and starvation for ever. Then she turned to the red bitch and thrashed her for her negligence, calling her lazy, useless, good-for-nothing.

But on another occasion, not so long afterwards, she was glad that the two dogs had stayed inside. At this end of the village the night had been quiet, but in the Untouchable quarter to the west, there'd been quite a kerfuffle. No one had heard the jackals howling, but the dogs, alerted to something, had barked and barked. Then, just before dawn, the barking had given way to the growls and scrabbling sounds of a fight.

When the first people left for the fields in the morning they found a dead dog on the path. It was lying on its side with its legs drawn stiffly up to a grossly distended belly. The jaw hung slightly open and the lips, peeled back in a snarl, displayed two rows of perfect teeth, the pink tip of a tongue, and a mouthful of blood-tinged white froth. The dog was rabid.

Word spread quickly and very soon a crowd had gathered. Some of the men wore striped, yak's-wool blankets draped over their heads and the shoulders of their thick woollen jackets. The morning was bitterly cold and their breath formed clouds of steam as they stared and muttered. No one approached the dog; it lay in a space of its own with its head and shoulders displayed on the icy stones of the path, its hindquarters crouched in the frosty grass. When a young boy, overcome with curiosity, stepped out and prodded the dog's mouth with a stick, he was grabbed by the arm and hauled back roughly; and when a dog began idly sniffing the body, someone kicked out and shouted and it lurched away through the crowd.

Some time later a Ḍum leatherworker dragged away the body and buried it, and at the headman's house a group of men had gathered around the fire, talking. The rabid dog was not from here and no one knew a dog like it – big and black, with white on its chest and ears, and raw sores around the nose and eyes. But yesterday it was seen in Chaura and in Chhuma, running through the outskirts of the villages; and the day before, a dog like that had chased a sheep in Pere, and clutched it by the neck, shaking it from one side to the other until it died of shock.

Everyone knew the tales of rabid dogs: how they suddenly went wild and uncontrollable, spinning round in circles, and rampaging through a village scattering chickens, or baying at the moon and running with the jackals. And everyone knew of the people they'd bitten, like the man who went mad – wandering round the village in search of water, complaining of aching limbs and an unquenchable thirst – and whose body was found, months later, washed up in the river at Lāmri.

130

The men at the headman's house decided, on behalf of the village, that every dog that had been out in the night, possibly taking part in the fight and helping bring down the rabid dog, would have to be killed; and all bitches on heat, whether they'd been inside or out, must also be killed. Anyone who'd paid money for their dog, or didn't know where it had been, should take it to the god in Lāmri to be blessed and cured; and if anyone had been bitten recently, or had been in contact with the rabid dog, they too should see that god.

In the days that followed many dogs were led through the village on their way to Lāmri. They came from Chaura and from Chhuma, from Huri, Muri, Pere and from Gorigāuṅ – the mad dog on its final rampage had run for miles, and in every village the dogs had scrapped and wrangled with it.

No one knew how the Lāmri god acquired his reputation for treating mad dogs, but it dated back for several generations. The god had been incarnated in five successive *dhāmis*, possessing each one during seances for the whole of his adult life. When one *dhāmi* died the god chose another and was embodied in him so that, although *dhāmis* came and went, the god's reputation endured. His power was said to be so great that each one of the *dhāmis*, when possessed by him, could split an iron cooking tripod with a single blow of his naked hand.

The *ḍāṅgri* took his mastiff mongrel together with a parcel of rice for the *dhāmi*; when he returned in the evening he said that the dog was no longer afflicted. The *dhāmi*, possessed by the god, had exorcized its sickness, stroking its head and back with an eagle's wing, then sprinkling rice grains while muttering a blessing.

But many more dogs were slaughtered. Not everyone destroyed the puppies in their dogs' litters, as Kalchu had done with the red bitch's, and there were any number of dogs that belonged to no one – wandering through the village, scavenging what they could find, breeding and multiplying. Almost all of these pariahs, as well as many household dogs, were killed.

It was mainly the young boys who did the slaughtering. They led the dogs to a place where the river meandered and the shingle bank was broad and deserted, and they beat them with sticks or stoned them. The carcasses were left to rot; vultures and buzzards patrolled the sky, homing in on tattered wings. When the wind was wrong, the putrid stench was wafted up across the fields.

During that time few people left the village at night. They were scared of the dogs that had been bitten and strayed; scared that the jackals, gone mad, would come in from the forest and molest them in packs. At the crossroads outside the village a row of clay effigies had been placed by those who'd been bitten. They were rough clay self-likenesses on to which the suspected disease was transferred. And at night the disease, thus disembodied, could adhere to anyone wandering past.

But, in due course, life returned to normal. No one in the village had contracted any symptoms. The dogs that remained seemed more contented, better fed, and presented a less impenetrable front of barking to strangers passing through. Memories died; and the dead dogs' bones, picked bare by the vultures, had been scattered on the shingle or swept into the river now flooded with melted mountain snow.

When spring had come, the village filled for a week or so with men from the Tibetan villages further north. They'd spent the winter working in India or the bazaar towns on the border and were returning now to their wives and children and their homes. Some still wore traditional clothing: sheepskin *chubas* slung rakishly over one shoulder, heavy turquoise and silver hoop earrings, embroidered knee-length boots. But most of them wore Western dress: polyester trousers, anoraks and sneakers. They were trading in the village, bartering orange plastic beads and metalware that they'd bought in India for flour and grain.

Kalchu's trading partner, his *iṣṭa*, from Wangri stayed in the house for several days. Their two families had exchanged hospitality and traded with one another for generations, when Kalchu's went north for its salt and his *iṣṭa*'s came south for grain. Most of the time their relationship was friendly and relaxed; in the daytime they went about their separate business and at night they came back to eat and sleep.

But one day a row blew up. Everyone else was out at work, and the two of them were sitting inside in the semi-darkness drinking *raksi*. The Tibetan was talking in loud self-congratulatory tones about the religious statues and paintings that he'd smuggled across the border and sold in India; how time and again he'd outwitted the border police, with silver, musk and contraband of every sort. Most of his relatives, he said, traded in Bangkok and Singapore now, and everyone had a watch, a radio and money to spend.

Kalchu was sitting quietly, staring at the ground. The Tibetan, growing ugly and aggressive, and slurring his speech, said that the trouble with Kalchu – like everyone else round here – was that he was ignorant, backward. He knew nothing about the world – his children didn't even go to school. All he did, day in day out, was sweat and slog in the fields, and even then there was never enough to eat.

It was true that at this altitude – where crops could be grown but only with constant attention – people were slaves to their land. Further north and higher in the mountains, where most of the Tibetans lived, the land was virtually barren and people had been forced into trade. So paradoxically, those with the poorest land came in the end to prosper the most.

Kalchu, his face red from alcohol and anger, his breath coming in short shallow gasps, said that he'd lived and worked in India for several years and that there he'd been nothing. With no home, no land, he was miserable, lost. He stood up suddenly, kicking his empty bowl of *raksi* and, shouting abuse at the Tibetan, made for the door. The Tibetan followed him outside. For a moment it seemed he would hit him, then the violence passed from his face and his arms relaxed.

But the red bitch, who'd been standing nearby, had sensed the aggression and, all of a sudden, crouching low to the ground and snarling, she lunged towards him. The Tibetan intuitively spun on his heel, raising his arm as if to throw a stone and bellowing great roars of abuse. But it was too late. The red bitch's jaws were clamped to his leg in an iron grip and she'd no intention of letting him go.

Immediately Kalchu rushed over, shouting at the red bitch to get back, kicking and thumping her. Eventually he pulled her off and dragged her away by the scruff of her neck. She was still growling warningly and when the Tibetan, incensed with rage, lunged for her, she flared up again, snarling viciously and struggling free of Kalchu's grasp. But the Tibetan had no strength for revenge; the blood had drained from his head and he slumped to the ground, clutching his leg. The wound was swollen and livid; the colours of bruising were showing already and a triangle of loose flesh shrouded a gaping red wound.

Crowds of people had gathered around: Chola and the twins, back from the fields, Sigarup, Kāli, Nara and Mina, all were staring, aghast. Some of the older men began moving the children aside, giving instructions and taking control.

Recovering now, the Tibetan stood up and, dragging his wounded leg in its shredded covering of black polyester, he lurched his way over to Kalchu. Standing directly in front of him, his face calm and assured, he demanded five hundred rupees as compensation.

Kalchu refused. Again their voices rose in hostility, neither one relenting, and when violence was threatened, four or five men stepped in, restraining them. Arguments followed. Chola took Kalchu's side, saying that the red bitch had never harmed anyone before, that if the Tibetan had provoked her it was his own fault. But some of the other men supported the Tibetan: within his own home Kalchu was responsible for his dog's behaviour. Eventually it was decided that if Kalchu refused to pay the money the Tibetan should be allowed to kill the dog.

The effects of the *raksi* had worn off by now and Kalchu, quiet and subdued, went into the house to fetch the red bitch's chain.

She too was calm and stood patiently while he attached the chain to a length of rope around her neck. When he led her away down the back steps the Tibetan followed and so did most of the crowd.

I put the puppy inside, closing the doors, and sat down on the roof. Voices rose from the waste-ground at the back of the house – they were discussing how to chain up the dog. Soon afterwards the yelping began. First came the clashing sound of stone against stone and the resounding thud of boulders dropped to the ground; then the recurrent frantic yelping. Sometimes I could hear the chain clanking as the red bitch moved around, running in one direction, and then, as the chain pulled her up, turning about. And sometimes, when the heaviest boulders thumped to the ground, I could feel the reverberations jolting the house.

At last there was silence. I watched the Tibetan walk casually out of the village. Then, turning back, I caught sight of the red bitch; she was making her way slowly towards the woodpile. Neither of her back legs was functioning and she dragged them painstakingly behind her, taking all the weight on her front legs, her head hung low. The Tibetan hadn't killed her. He'd mutilated her to the point of death but – being a Buddhist – he hadn't killed her.

All through that evening I pleaded with Kalchu to shoot her, but he wouldn't, or couldn't – none of us could. At one point I took a bowl of water to her; her mouth was bleeding and a trail of saliva dangled from her lower lip. She ignored the water. After that I avoided looking down towards the woodpile until, when it was almost too dark to see, I glanced down one last time – and she was gone.

All of us assumed that she'd wandered off to die alone and that, sooner or later, we'd come across her body, sprawled in a ditch or hidden from view in a clump of thorn trees. But that night as we sat around the fire no one mentioned it. Kalchu was ashamed of his drunkenness and Chola grumbled and rebuked him for it, but no one regretted its effect on the red bitch or mourned her loss. The children chattered and squabbled as usual, and the puppy, pleased with its solitary status, snapped up all the food that was offered and licked out all the plates by itself. I went to bed feeling hollow – removed from the people I lived with.

But the following morning I awoke to the familiar sound of Chola shouting at the dogs and the dogs' yelping response. The red bitch had returned, as insistent on food as ever, and limping only slightly as she trotted around, getting in the way, impeding Chola's cooking.

When the Tibetan returned some months later he was impressed that the red bitch had survived. Joking with Kalchu, he said he could do with a guard dog like that, fierce and resilient. And so when he set off for home the red bitch was with him, loping along by his side.

TWO GENERATIONS OF HUNTING

AFTER THE POTATO HARVEST IN NOVEMBER THERE WAS NO MORE work to be done in the fields until the ploughing began in early spring. Sometimes groups of women would leave the village and climb the surrounding hillsides, cutting bundles of grass to feed to the cattle in the winter. Sometimes men and women would go to the forest to gather firewood – building up the piles against the cold months to come. But often people stayed at home, finding jobs to do around the house.

One day I was sitting on the roof with Chola and Mina, shelling wild walnuts for oil. The afternoon sun on my back was gently warming and the light that it cast on Chola's and Mina's faces was as clear and richly brown as amber. To open the walnuts we placed them on one stone and hammered with another. Many were so hard that they seemed to be made of solid wood while others shattered like eggshells, but were virtually empty. We had been sitting there since early that morning, cracking the nuts, picking out the flesh with needles.

Below us in the village square Kalchu had pegged out his backstrap loom and was weaving a length of grey goat's-hair cloth to make a rug. A group of men had gathered round him, smoking *chillims*, talking. Some of them had brought their wooden spindles and, from time to time, they abstractedly twisted them, spinning coils of fluffy wool into a smooth yarn as they talked or listened. From where we sat we could hear their occasional bursts of laughter and the dim drone of their voices, but the words themselves were lost to us.

When the sun had finally disappeared behind the mountain Chola stood up to go and light a fire inside the house. She'd almost reached the door when suddenly a gunshot sounded, shattering the stillness. For an instant its echo rippled through the valley.

Then another shot was fired and the two echoes clashed discordantly.

Immediately the gathering of men disbanded. Kalchu came rushing up the notched-pole ladder. 'It's a boar hunt,' he shouted. 'I'm going to go and have a look.' He hurried through the open doorway into the house and a few seconds later reappeared carrying a rifle which he passed from one hand to the other as he struggled into his jacket. He was already half-way down the ladder when he shouted back at me, 'Don't you want to come along, sister?' For a split second I hesitated, uncertain. Then I grabbed my jacket and followed him.

From the path below I looked back towards the house. Chola and Mina were at the edge of the roof watching the stream of men as they poured from the village. Some were running; some were striding purposefully; some had rifles slung across their shoulders on rope straps. Dogs ran in and out among their feet, barking, or with noses down, tails streaming, sniffed the ground for the boar's scent, knowing instinctively that this was a hunt.

The shots had sounded from the hills somewhere to the north, and rather than wasting time on the main path that rose with the gentle contours of the valley, we took a short cut up the steep, almost sheer, cliff behind the houses. I followed Kalchu as he pushed his way into the line of men climbing in single file up the roughly carved, foot-sized steps, but most of the men simply scaled the slope, holding on to roots and tufts of grass.

At the top of the cliff we paused to catch our breath and look around. From here we could see for quite a distance, but there was no sign of the hunt, nor any sound. So we set out across the open grassy slope that led on up towards the forest.

At first the forest too was silent, apart from the men's voices calling out to one another as they searched for tracks. But then another gunshot sounded, much closer than the first and as loud as thunder overhead. The men immediately set off in one direction, scrambling down through the trees and undergrowth towards the subsidiary valley where the shot had sounded.

Minutes later, although we could still see nothing through the trees, we heard the dogs' excited, nearly frantic, barking. Another single shot was fired and, above the shrill ringing in our ears as the blast subsided, there rose a high-pitched, almost human, scream.

Finally, as we approached the edge of the forest where the trees were thinner, we glimpsed the hunt. Crowds of men were standing on the river-bank, pushing and jostling, craning their necks and shifting position, trying to get a view through the mass of bodies and out across the water. The dogs, too, were focused on the water, poised on the edge of the bank, barking and snarling, or pacing back and forth between the men's legs, whining with impatience.

I followed Kalchu behind the crowd to a place where there were fewer people and we could go right up to the water's edge. Looking back from here along the river, we saw the boar. It had been wounded, and was struggling to stay afloat with its snout jutting horizontally above the water, its dark mane of bristle bobbing up and down amid the white rise of the current. Suddenly the crowd started to stone it. When the first stones hurtled towards the boar, it lunged forward, its head rising clear above the water so that we could see the downward curve of its tusks, the bead-like eyes wild with terror. For a moment it seemed as though it had tapped some hidden reserve of strength and would ease itself up on to the opposite bank, and escape into the forest. But then another shot was fired. The boar keeled over instantly, and the water that flowed away downstream was a pale rusty brown.

The relief among the crowd was almost palpable. People began to move about, the hum of their voices sweeping like a wave along the bank. A faint smell of gunpowder still hung in the air and a trail of bluish smoke drifted off towards the forest.

Within minutes, five or six men had taken off their shoes, rolled up their trousers and were wading in the icy water. Some of the dogs, too, had slithered down from the bank and were swimming out towards the boar. Everyone watched as the water reached the top of the men's thighs, then their hips, before finally becoming shallower again as they passed the mid-point in the river and approached the opposite bank. For a while they just stood there, staring down at the boar, satisfying their curiosity after the brief and distant glimpses that they'd had on the hunt. Then they became animated, gesturing and talking, devising a strategy to bring the boar back across the river.

Reaching into the water they grabbed hold of the boar's legs, and after several attempts swivelled it over on to its back. While some of the men held the weight of the body in place, others bound the forelegs, and the hind legs, together with rope. Some then leaned on the rope, hauling the boar through the water, while others stayed behind to guide it round rocks and counteract the drag of the current. When they were close enough they threw the ropes up to the men at the front of the crowd, and all of them pushed from behind. With one concerted effort, they heaved the boar out of the water and up on to the bank.

Immediately the men homed in on the dead animal with the single-mindedness of monsoon flies. I waited for the crowd to thin out, then went to have a closer look. The boar was much bigger than I'd thought. It was stretched out on the grass; standing, it would have almost reached my waist. There were two bullet wounds, one on the shoulder and a deeper one behind the head. Dark blood was welling up from both of them. For one brief moment I felt the full shock of its death; of a life, until recently, so remote, so inextricably part of the mountains and forests, now suddenly laid out at my feet.

Looking up, I saw that night had almost fallen. The shapes of the pine trees on the far side of the river were already indistinguishable; the forest had become a dark impenetrable expanse that stretched from the water's edge right up to the horizon. The river too was uniformly dark apart from the ripples and eddies which were thin ribbons of light.

I turned back towards the crowd. Some of the men had been collecting driftwood and dry sticks and branches from among the trees; a small fire was coming to life, crackling and spluttering sparks into the haze of heat above it. Soon its warmth would be welcome; the night air was cold and the grass on the river-bank was already crisp with frost.

I looked around for Kalchu and eventually found him on the far side of the fire talking to a group of men, some of whom I recognized as being from Chaura and from Chhuma. He was asking them how the hunt had begun, and what had happened before we joined it.

'We started out from Chaura,' one of them began, 'early, before the sun was up. For hours we searched the forests on the western slopes – nothing. Then, just as we were about to give up, the dogs picked up a scent. Moments later two boars came crashing through the undergrowth. Someone fired a shot but the trees were too thick to see properly and the boars ran out of the forest on to the open plateau above. We could see them clearly then, a male and a female, full-grown adults. Someone fired again and the boars split up. The female shot off into the forest and was lost; the male dropped straight down into the valley, right into the arms of the rest of the hunting party waiting here with guns.'

Kalchu was reflecting, wondering which of the shots we'd heard from the house. I turned towards the boar again. By the light of the fire the butchering had begun. I watched as one of the men, squatting down by the boar, made a deep incision along the underside from chest to groin, then hacked through the ribs and breast-bone with an adze. When the carcass was opened the men called over the dogs, which cowered back uncertainly. For a few seconds they encouraged the dogs to sniff and lick the blood – to reaffirm their hunting instinct – then, shouting and waving their arms, they sent them scurrying back to the shadows to wait for bones and other bits of debris.

Kalchu told me later that the butchering and apportioning of meat strictly follows precedent. The legs belong to the men who've organized the hunt. These are almost always the same men, the ones who own the guns and the best-trained dogs, whose families have been hunters for years, passing their knowledge and experience down through the generations until it's almost in the blood. They also get the tusks and the bristles which they sell or barter in India, and a large proportion of the fat, which can be rendered down and used for cooking, or dried and preserved to smear on cuts and bruises. The rest of the meat is divided up among all those present at the kill – the reason being that it's only by sheer force of numbers that any hunt succeeds.

Five or six young boys had come over to the fire with some scraps of meat and sections of cleaned intestine that they skewered with sticks and laid on the embers to roast. Every now and again they checked its progress, tilting their faces back from the heat as they reached into the core of the fire. When the meat had shrivelled and curled they waved the sticks in the cold air for a minute, unskewered it, blew off the coating of ash and tossed it from hand to hand until it was cool enough to eat.

Soon pieces of meat were being roasted right around the fire, and the air was thick with the smell of charred flesh and singeing fur. Someone leaned down in front of me with his cupped palms outstretched. I helped myself to some of the raw still-warm liver he was offering, realizing that I was being especially honoured as a guest.

Much later when the butchering was finished, crowds of men stood arguing over the piles of meat. Apparently, most hunts begin and end high in the mountains, far away from any village, and all those present at the kill have been with the hunt throughout. Usually there are about twenty-five or thirty men, and an adult boar divided even forty ways provides a reasonable amount of meat for all. But today's hunt was close to home. Seventy or eighty men were at the kill and most of them, like us, had heard the shooting from their homes and hurried over just in time. Their claim to a share of the meat was bitterly resented.

When voices started rising and violence seemed inevitable, Kalchu told me that it wouldn't be resolved for hours and, rather than waiting around in the cold on the off-chance of getting some meat, we might as well set out for home.

The forest path was like the strange, disorientating setting of a nightmare. Tall trees and sweeping branches suddenly appeared from nowhere and vanished mysteriously into the all-encompassing darkness. Every sound seemed a potential threat – the wind rustling in the pine trees, the flapping of a startled bird's wings, the jackals' baleful howling as they patiently awaited the abandoned carcass. But Kalchu seemed familiar with the darkness and the narrow, winding path, and I followed as close behind him as I could.

When we left the forest, pale moonlight reflected dimly on the frosty ground and it was easier to see. Kalchu turned to me and, looking pleased with himself, opened out his *ṭopi* which was bulging full of meat. I hadn't noticed that he was carrying, not wearing, it and I certainly hadn't seen him take the meat.

The following morning it was snowing lightly – the first snow of winter. Kāli came to bring me some of the cooked meat, chewing some herself. She was very excited about the snow and the hunt.

'Weren't you ashamed last night?' she said half-critically. 'The only woman with all those men?'

'A bit,' I replied, 'but I'm very glad I went.'

We talked for a while about the hunt – she wanted to know how much meat we'd eaten, what the men had talked about – and then she said she had to go and graze the cows. Soon afterwards Chola and Mina set out for the hills to gather grass.

I went to sit with Kalchu and the children by the remains of their fire. It was still snowing outside, and so cold that Kalchu decided, despite the extravagance, to build up the fire and keep it alight right through the day. Kalchu's brother and several other men, seeing the smoke from outside, came to share the warmth of one of the few fires still burning. Kalchu shut the door behind them. The room was warm and dark and filled with smoke. The only daylight came through a chink between the heavy wooden doors. Kalchu fetched a bottle of *raksi* from the inner room and filled a bowl for each of us. Inevitably the conversation turned to hunting.

'If only the hunting now was like it used to be when we were their age,' said Kalchu, nodding towards the twins. 'In those days our fathers and grandfathers kept us well provided. There was always meat to eat: fresh meat after every hunt, dried meat in between.'

'But why was it so much better then?' I asked, wondering if it really was or if his memory had become glamorized.

'Well, for a start,' he explained, 'everyone had a gun. The blacksmith used to make them for us out of wood and steel that we carried back from India. He used to make the bullets too, little strips of iron that he heated, twisted, battered into shape. They're the same guns – and bullets – that we use today, but in the whole village, only about seven or eight of them are left.'

'What happened to all the others?' I asked, curious now.

'Oh, one day, quite a few years ago' – Kalchu's tone was flat with resignation – 'the Bazaar police came, issuing orders that from now on all firearms must be licensed. They went around from house to house demanding the licensing fee. You could either pay ten rupees or, if you didn't have the money, you could give a chicken, or three households together could give a sheep. Almost all of us refused and they tore our houses apart and seized the guns.

'Usually,' he went on, 'when there's to be a police raid of any sort we know about it before it happens. Someone hears it mentioned in the Bazaar and runs to Uṭhu with a warning. Then, from Uṭhu, someone else sets off for Lāmri and for Lorpa. Eventually the news will reach us here, and one of us will go to Chaura and to Chhuma and to Gorigāuṅ. They shouldn't have found a single gun that day – we'd have buried the lot if we'd only known in time.'

'So where are all the guns now?' I asked.

Kalchu shrugged. 'They took them back to the barracks in the

Bazaar. Maybe they're still there – a great heap of them going rusty and covered in dust and cobwebs. They're no use to anyone in the Bazaar, they all have modern rifles now. When they took them away they said we could come and reclaim them any time we wanted, if we brought ten rupees. No one ever went.'

The new wood that Kalchu had put on the fire earlier hadn't caught yet and clouds of smoke were billowing out. His brother Māilo leaned forward, rearranged the logs and blew on them. Within seconds the smoke had cleared and a flame shot up, strong and high.

'Then some years after that,' Kalchu continued absentmind- edly, as though the story had its own momentum like a ball set rolling down a hill, 'the Bazaar police came back. This time they told us that we were to stop hunting musk and *tār*. They said the government had declared them "protected species" and that killing them was now a criminal offence. At first we didn't take any notice, we just carried on regardless. But we soon learned that the police have eyes and ears everywhere – every village, every forest, every mountain.'

Lāla Bahādur's desultory grizzling, which for some time had provided a steady accompaniment to his father's voice, suddenly broke into an urgent heartfelt wail. Kalchu reached over to where he and Hārkini had been squabbling, picked him up by both elbows and pulled him on to his lap. Heavy tears were brimming from his eyes, washing clear channels through the dirt and grime. For a minute or two all conversation was silenced while Kalchu bounced him on his lap and muttered softly through his screaming.

When at last the child was comforted, Māilo looked up at me across the fire. 'You wouldn't believe the amount of meat we'd bring back when we hunted *tār*.' His eyes were bright with reflections of the flames. 'Mountains of it. There was so much that we used to cut it into strips and string it from the eaves to dry in the wind and sun. We had to sit there watching it for days to keep away the dogs and chickens and stop the crows and vultures swooping down and snatching it away.'

Suddenly his smile faded and he hugged his body, grimacing. 'But it was always so bitterly cold. You can only hunt *tār* in the autumn and the winter. In the summer they go right up into the mountains, way beyond the permanent snow-line. It's too dangerous to hunt them there among all those crags and chasms full of drifted snow. But in the autumn they come down and settle in the grazing pastures where we take the sheep in summer.

'That's where we used to go to hunt them. Often we'd stalk a herd for days on end, and all that time we'd never even catch a glimpse. We just followed footprints in the snow and sometimes, in the morning when the air was still, we'd think we heard them not too far away. At night we'd sleep in caves, huddled up in blankets with nothing to burn for firewood, while outside an icy wind swirled clouds of snow-dust all around us.

'But we'd always get one in the end. We used to chase them down a narrow valley with a sheer cliff-wall at the end.' He cocked his head, half-smiling. 'They're cunning animals but they're used to being hunted by leopards, not by men with guns. What they do then is scale a cliff, clambering from one ledge to another until they're perched on one so high and narrow that the leopard can't follow. It goes as far as it can and waits there for a while, its big eyes staring up, tantalized. Then it loses heart and goes away. But what the *tār* doesn't realize is that it makes a perfect target for a gun, stuck up there with its pale fur as clearly visible against the dark rock as the moon is in the sky at night.'

Māilo's eyes always had a disconcerting twinkle; whatever he was saying I was never sure if he was teasing me. Now for a moment I wondered if he'd made the entire story up – the elusive animal, the bizarre hunting technique. 'What do they look like – *tār*?' I asked by way of checking.

'They're a sort of greyish-brown colour,' he said ambiguously, 'a bit like a deer. A bit like our goats, only much much bigger.'

At that point Kalchu stood up, rummaged round behind the

9. Mina and her baby.

10. The *ḍāṅgri* smoking a *chillim.*

11. Kalchu winnowing.

12. The potato harvest, with potatoes baking in a brushwood fire.

13. The village path in the early morning.

14. Saumi, Kāli
and Lāla Bahādur.

15. *Kāmi* boys drumming.

16. Bānchu, Jakali's eldest daughter.

rafters and, after a while, pulled out a dusty horn which he handed me. I looked at it and ran my fingers down its spiral-patterned surface. 'A *tār* horn,' he said, and a moment later added, 'that's how the hunters carry their gunpowder: fill it up, stuff the top with a birch-bark bung and tie it to their rifle straps.'

Everyone watched me, pleased that I seemed impressed. Then a man I didn't know who was sitting next to me nudged me in the ribs. 'One year,' he said, when he was sure of my attention, 'the shepherds found a *tār* when they were crossing the high ridge on their way back from Aula in the spring. There it was, just lying there, half-buried in the snow. They thought that it could only just have died. It was big and fleshy and the vultures hadn't touched it – even the eyes were still in place. But when they had a closer look they saw that it was frozen solid. It must have been killed in an avalanche or died in a blizzard earlier in the winter. But it was quite uncanny – three days earlier it would have been completely covered in snow and they'd never have seen it; three days later it would have been stripped to a skeleton.' He paused for a minute. Then he added, 'Nowadays, when the shepherds come back that way in spring, they prod every square inch of snow with sticks in search of buried frozen *tār*.' Everyone laughed at this. 'They'll never learn,' he said, 'that luck like that can only happen once.'

Kalchu stood up and went to fetch another bottle of *raksi*. When he came back several minutes later, he was still smiling. All of us watched as he poured some of the clear liquid into each of our bowls and then began kneading the tobacco to put in a *chillim*.

'If they hadn't stopped us hunting musk,' said Māilo, knocking the spent tobacco out of the *chillim* on the side of the hearth, 'we'd probably all be rich by now. And the beauty of hunting musk was that you didn't even need a gun.' He passed the emptied *chillim* over to Kalchu. 'All we had to do was take a basketful of poison-tipped bamboos into the mountains and stake them diagonally into the ground, right across the width of the valley. Then it was up to us and the dogs to stalk a herd and chase them in the right direction. If everything worked the deer would kill themselves, impaling their bodies on the wall of bamboo stakes. We'd usually get at least five or six that way.

'One year' – Mäilo's eyes lit up at the memory – 'I sold so many musk pods at the Indian border that I could hardly walk back, my pockets were so weighted down with silver coins.'

Kalchu searched in the fire for an ember, laid it on top of the *chillim* and drew in deeply. When he breathed out again his face was lost for a moment in the smoke. He inhaled once more and passed the *chillim* on. 'Now that it's illegal,' he said, coughing, 'it's worth a thousand times what it used to fetch. All those Tibetans who come back from India in the spring laden down with watches, silver jewellery, radios – where do you think they get their money from?' It was a comment directed more to the other men than to me.

'Ye-es,' the man next to me agreed, 'but it's madness unless you've got the money to bribe the right officials. They caught someone in the Bazaar just the other day. He only had a little bit, but they put him away for three years. If it had been at the border they'd have given him five or even ten.'

Mäilo suddenly started to laugh. 'Gone are the days when we used to crumble half a *tola* of it into a *chillim* of tobacco.'

'Why did you do that?' I asked. 'Does it make you high like marijuana?'

'Oh no. It just makes it smell and taste ... mm, wonderful.'

'They'll never stamp it out completely,' said Kalchu confidently. 'In fact, if you ask me, there's as much goes on in most of these valleys as there ever used to be.' He turned to the man beside me. 'Last monsoon when I needed some musk to rub on a snake-bite, I didn't have to look far. True, everyone had hidden their supplies – buried them in the tobacco patch or the bottom of the grain chest – and I had to convince them that I wasn't a forester. But there was no shortage of it; and it wasn't all old and dry like walnuts, it was as fresh and sweetly-smelling as the day the deer was slain.

'And that dog that was gored by a boar this time last year,' he went on, 'the one that they carried home and looked after like a baby for days until, in the end, it died. That was no ordinary dog, that was a trained musk-hunter. They bought that dog in Tibet for five thousand rupees.'

'Where there's money to be made you can bet there's someone making it,' said an old man who'd been silently working his spindle since the conversation began.

Kalchu poured out the remains of the *raksi* into two or three empty bowls and put some more wood on the fire.

'You know what I think about this "protected species" business,' he said, reshuffling the logs, 'I think they're protecting all the game for themselves so they can set up a hunter's paradise for the rich – for foreigners and high-ranking government officials. They're probably going to buy up all our land and evacuate us to the south, or let us stay and employ us all as beaters.'

I'd heard some of the other men in the village mention the possibility of a game reserve for tourists, and I held my breath, wondering if Kalchu was going to implicate me, as they had done. But he was in a cheerful mood and he went on with another story altogether. 'When we were boys – Nara's age – the king arrived in the valley with his hunting party in seven helicopters. They paid the headman of the village five hundred rupees and all of us had to streak through the forest making as much noise as we possibly could to round up the game. The king and his party had a feast at the edge of the forest. There were tables with white cloths and chicken, rice, *raksi*, sweets – everything. We watched it all through the trees. Then when they'd finished eating they picked up their guns and the animals were there, ready and waiting. Bang, bang, bang. They did very well on that day.'

The door opened, letting in a flood of light, and Kāli walked in. Her shawl was tightly wrapped round her head and shoulders. It was dark with moisture and dotted with white flecks of snow. She went over to the fire and squatted down beside the twins, warming her hands and bare feet. Most of the men got up to leave, shocked that the day had passed so quickly, that the cows were home already.

I went out on to the roof, glad to be in the fresh air after the smoky room and the *raksi*. Snow was falling as steadily as the apricot blossom in the first monsoon storm. But it wasn't cold enough to settle. After a whole day there was just a thin layer of muddy slush.

As winter took its hold, banking up the short days, the long cold nights between autumn and spring, thoughts and imaginations often drifted to hunting. The craving for meat seemed to grow with the cold; chickens were sometimes killed and eaten but never gratuitously, only in sacrifice at the gods' demand, and the sheep and goats were away in the south. Nara, like most of the other young boys, laid noose traps in the snow for birds. He once caught a pigeon, but it was mostly sparrows so small that, when he laid them on the embers to cook, they were ready by the time the feathers had singed and were hardly worth even sharing, except with the twins who insisted.

And almost every time a group of men sat round together – inside by someone's fire at night, or when it snowed; outside in the sun, when the sky was clear – they talked about going hunting. But for one reason or another their plans were never carried out. Then, towards the end of January, people noticed that at least one boar was coming right up to the village in its night-time foraging; there were tracks in the snow and patches of scratched earth where it had been digging for roots. One morning, someone found his potato-storage pit on the corner of his land ransacked and emptied. It was this that finally resolved the men to organize a hunt.

When Kalchu and I set out for the headman's house several mornings later it was bitterly cold. The mud on the path was frozen as hard as baked clay. Snow from the last fall, several weeks previously, still lay packed in straw- and grit-speckled drifts on the sunless north-facing sides of the houses and thorn bush hedges. Kalchu was wearing his rope-soled woollen boots and a red, brown and yellow striped blanket wrapped around his shoulders. I had on my down-jacket, zipped and buttoned to my chin, and a pair of leather walking-boots.

The headman's house was already full of men, warming themselves and talking round the central fire. We stood in the doorway for a while until our eyes adjusted to the darkness and then, stooping low to avoid the worst of the smoke, we made our way through the crowd to a space that had been cleared for us close to the fire. One or two of the men greeted Kalchu with nods and comments and several of them expressed surprise that I was coming with them.

On the far side of the hearth the headman was sitting with his legs crossed, his back very straight, ceremoniously smoking a hookah. Each time he drew on the mouthpiece, setting in motion the gentle protracted gurgle, he stared into space, completely absorbed. Some of the other men were worrying, expressing doubts about the weather, wondering if the hunt should be postponed. The forests, they said, were still deep in snow and, judging by the way the wind was stirring, there'd be another heavy fall before the day was out. Eventually the headman passed on the hookah stem and stood up, saying he'd go and fetch the soothsayer.

When the two of them appeared in the doorway some time later, several of the men shuffled along to make a welcoming space by the fire. The soothsayer sat down, nodding in general greeting, and held out his hands to the warmth. Soon afterwards the headman came out of the inner room, carrying a plate of rice grains which he put on the ground beside him.

For some time the soothsayer continued to warm himself, staring into the flames. Then, without a word, he picked up the plate and tossed a stream of rice grains into the air. When they'd landed back on the plate, he leaned forward, studying the pattern they'd formed. Everyone was watching in silence, awaiting his verdict.

He put the plate back on the ground and looked up. His eyes were the greyish-green of pine needles. When at last he started to speak it was with his hands, in sign language. Some of the men asked questions and made comments, also in sign language, and I asked Kalchu what they were saying. 'There's no danger,' he translated, his eyes on the soothsayer's hands, 'but the boar that we want is as fast as the wind and as sharp as an eagle.' He paused and then added, 'In any case, everyone thinks we should go.'

When we left the headman's house we were joined by a group of young boys who'd been waiting outside with their dogs, and by other men from houses that we passed along the way. All the men wore thick scarves wrapped around their heads and ears against the cold; the sky had darkened to the colour of a brownish-yellow bruise and the smell of snow was unmistakable.

Walking fairly briskly at first to keep the fire's warmth with us, we went down through the fields, crossed the main bridge and followed a tributary upstream until the valley narrowed out. Then one of the men shouted something, waving his arms in the general direction of the forest. Everyone stopped and looked around and one or two voices shouted back to him along the valley. Then the young boys and some of the men split off, leading their dogs on chains up a steep animal track that climbed straight to the heart of the forest.

The rest of us watched them disappear among the trees and then continued on the broader path, climbing slowly. Kalchu explained that every hunt begins like this: the dogs flush out the forest – the inaccessible chasms and the narrow hidden valleys – and when they've found a boar, they're trained to chase it downhill only. So, if things go right, the men below should know from the dogs' barking where the boar is coming out and be waiting with their guns to ambush it.

We'd heard the dogs' barking spreading through the trees when they'd first been unleashed. But they were out of earshot now. We were walking through a silent forest. The snow on the path in front of us was flawless; behind, it was as churned up as a freshly-harrowed field. In time the first snowflakes fluttered down between the trees.

I was surprised that the pace of a hunt could be so leisurely. The men were ambling along, stopping every now and then for rests, biding time until their turn came round.

At one point they stopped to smoke a *chillim* in a glade where the conifers were thinner and dense clumps of feathery-leafed bamboo had spread across the open spaces. Although it was mid-winter now, the glade was as freshly green as the birch woods are in early summer.

While we were waiting for the *chillim* to be filled and passed around, Kalchu pointed out a conical heap of stones at the base of a great cedar tree near the edge of the glade. He told me that it was a shrine to Ban Bhāi, god of the forest. There was a time, he said, when every hunting party had sacrificed a chicken here. If they didn't make the offering – if they plundered the god's territory without his permission – he'd punish their families with sickness or even death. But now, he said, no one bothered any more. Five or six stones had toppled from the pile and were lying half-buried in the snow, and some red and white cloth streamers that had been tied to a branch of the tree fluttered slightly in the breeze, torn and faded from the wind and rain.

Suddenly, as we were walking on, we heard the dogs barking in that frantic, menacing way that could only mean they'd given chase. The men paused in their tracks, locating the sound, and within seconds we were hurrying back to a place that we'd passed where the sheer slope of the mountain was broken only by the deep rift of a water-course. This, they said, was the only route for the boar to take.

The barking grew louder. They were definitely coming this way. The men positioned themselves with their guns ready and were straining to see, scanning the length and breadth of the forested gully. But it was still too soon, there was nothing to see, no movement in the branches, no rippling streak through the trees.

All of a sudden, mixed with the excitement, which was inevitable and contagious, I felt a strange weightlessness in the pit of my stomach. I remembered another story they'd told me that day of the first snowfall; it was about a hunt several years ago, on a day like this. The men had been in unknown country, chasing the boar uphill, when the rule is to chase downhill only. Suddenly, the boar had been faced with a cliff too steep to climb and had turned on its heel. The men, rooted to the ground in three feet of fresh snow, had been unable to move quickly enough, and the boar, finding its retreat blocked, had gone crazy and attacked indiscriminately. Six men had bled to death there in the snow or in the arms of friends and relatives as they carried them home.

And I remembered too the guns they'd shown me, with the barrels roughly brazed to patch holes that had been blasted-out by home-made bullets too misshapen to find a smooth passage through when the gun was fired. They told me that no one had ever been hurt like this; but wasn't it only a question of time?

The barking was getting closer by the second and we could hear the hunters whistling and shouting orders to the dogs, and the sound of the boar scrunching dried leaves and snapping dead branches as it hurtled down through the trees.

Then, unexpectedly, the barking stopped. A strange silence followed, as though the entire forest was listening, waiting. Occasionally one dog would bark in isolation; sometimes two or three more would join it. But the dogs were no longer working together, no longer a single-minded pack in close pursuit. Obviously they'd lost it.

The men stayed put for several minutes, hoping that it was just a temporary loss, but when the silence continued they began to move about, rubbing their hands together to warm them up, making light of their disappointment with careless shrugs of the shoulders and wry half-smiles. Someone filled and lit a *chillim* and everyone gathered round to smoke it, exchanging, now and then, laconic comments about the boar's escape, musing about what had happened and how different everything could have been if only luck was with them.

Then, looking up along the gully where the boar had been, Kalchu noticed a young boy leading his dog on a chain. As he approached we could see that the dog had been wounded; it was limping and the fur on its flank was matted with blood. The boy told us that his dog had been at the head of the pack from the start, biting the boar's heels and almost bringing it down. Then suddenly the boar had turned about and hurled it into the air. He said he was taking it home. When Kalchu asked him what the others would do, he confirmed our suspicion. It was cold, it would soon be dark, and the dogs were tired – they'd be following soon.

Some of the men had brought ropes and small axes with them so that, while they were in the forest, they could carry back a load of firewood rather than returning empty-handed if they didn't get the boar. We were far from any village now and there was plenty of dead wood just lying on the ground. As Kalchu and I and some of the other men set out for home, they started to gather it up and hack off the dead branches that jut out from pine-trunks like thin stumps of arms.

The snow was falling in earnest as we wound our way down through the trees, and the rich colours of the forest – the pine-green and henna-red bracken – were rapidly fading to ashen. For a long time the sound of the men chopping wood stayed with us. Eventually it was as faint as the steady tap-tap of a distant woodpecker.

Outside the forest the snow was already six inches deep and growing steadily, relentlessly deeper. As we turned into the open fields an icy wind rose, blustering flurries of snowflakes into our faces and eyes. I tilted my head down and tightened the cord on the hood of my jacket. For a long time I walked with my eyes on the ground, watching my feet sinking interminably into the snow.

When at last I looked up we'd almost arrived at the village. Blue smoke was billowing up through the snowflakes. The house would be warm; the women had probably started the cooking.

SOMETIMES WE'LL LAUGH AND SOMETIMES WE'LL CRY

THE WEDDING

ON THE WAY TO THE WEDDING KĀLI WAS VERY EXCITED. SHE WAS wearing her best clothes: a blue hand-printed skirt and a new cross-over jacket with great crimson and yellow flowers splashed luxuriantly over a dark blue background. She'd never been as far as Lāmri and was thrilled to be spending the night away from home. She talked about the food there'd be: *lāḍus* – special sweet-meats made for weddings; basketfuls of heavy golden *puris*; rice with curd or honey; maybe even meat.

When we got there the village seemed unnaturally quiet and we weren't sure where to go. We wandered down the central path and after a while came across two women fetching water. As they approached, Kāli fell resolutely silent, adjusting her shawl on her forehead, staring fixedly at the ground between us. I asked for the bridegroom's house and the women pointed us in the right direction, curious to know if we'd come all this way to see the wedding.

As we climbed the notched-pole ladder, blue smoke billowed through the open doorway, carrying the delicious doughy smell of *puris* frying. The group of women sitting on the roof were welcoming; they told us boastingly that an enormous wedding procession – almost all the men in the village, headed by the *Damāi* musicians with their kettledrums – had left the day before to fetch the bride from Moharigāuṅ. Then they introduced the bridegroom's grandmother – a distinguished-looking, white-haired woman sitting on a rug in the shade of the eaves – and his mother, vigorously grinding red beans between two flat stones to make the *dāl*.

One woman, laughingly, said we'd come too late. The best part of the celebrations had been the night before, when all the men were away in Moharigāuṅ, and the women had stayed awake till dawn, playing games and singing. They'd built a bonfire in the middle of the village and one of them had dressed up as a man – in trousers and a tunic, with her long hair stuffed into a *ṭopi* that kept on falling off – and pretended she was a deaf-mute, a cretin. The story broke off as everyone recalled the scene, reeling and spluttering first with laughter, then with coughing. Eventually they continued: this cretin had a pair of bells as testicles and a big mouli for a prick and he'd loped and staggered round, lunging out at women as he passed. When he captured one, he'd push her to the ground and hump her till she screamed and wailed and they both collapsed, convulsed with laughter.

Kāli had recovered from her shyness now and was chuckling openly. She turned to check my reaction. Her eyes met mine and for an instant we laughed together before our attention was once again claimed by the crowd.

All through the afternoon we could hear the wedding procession approaching; the kettledrums resounding, growing perceptibly louder, then temporarily receding, as the party wended its way through the hills and valleys, the fields and forests, between Moharigauṅ and Lāmri. The women worked hard. They finished frying the *puris* and put them to one side in baskets; they husked the rice and set it on the fire to boil in a huge copper vat; they peeled potatoes and ground salt, chilli and spices; they cooked and seasoned the *dāl*; and finally they plastered the house with a mud and cow-dung wash to make the house clean and ritually pure. Occasionally the bridegroom wandered in – a young boy, looking restless and bored, with his head newly shaven.

It was beginning to get dark when the procession finally approached the last stage of its journey. We could see it making its way down past the empty paddy fields, then turning to follow the broader path along the river bank. Kāli and I went down to the bridge and stood waiting amid a throng of children who were shouting and laughing, rowdy with anticipation.

The first to cross was the bridegroom's father, a haughty-looking man sitting tall on a white horse with a red-and-blue Tibetan saddle-blanket. His face, beneath the white turban, was proud and slightly arrogant as he stepped down off the bridge. Immediately he spurred his horse on, galloping ahead to announce their arrival. Clouds of dust rose in his tracks, enhancing the opulence of his black jacket against the horse's white coat, and of the horse's silvery tail streaming out behind.

Afterwards came the *Damāi* musicians, dramatic and exuberant in their wedding attire. Their kettledrums were suspended on straps across the shoulder so that they nestled against the body just below one hip, and as they marched they dexterously tumbled their drumsticks, beating out the rhythm on the great copper domes. They were wearing long white pleated skirts that flounced as they walked, and black sleeveless waistcoats over white shirts drawn tightly into cummerbunds at the waist. Red scarves were draped casually around their throats and they'd slotted marigolds into the folds of their turbans. As they crossed the bridge they flashed reckless smiles; their faces were brilliant – great vermilion *ṭikās* daubed between the eyes, white teeth gleaming from heavy black moustaches.

Then came the bride, carried on her uncle's back, with her arms loosely clasped around his throat. She was wearing a blue printed skirt, like Kāli's, and brown canvas shoes. Her head and upper body were swathed in shawls, an outer one of vivid sunshine yellow, and beneath it, showing through in places, a darker one of midnight blue. Her body was small and her uncle carried it effortlessly, stooping only slightly to counteract her weight. Following close behind were two young women, friends of the bride from Moharigāuṅ.

When they'd crossed the bridge the man unclasped his hands from underneath his niece's seat and gently helped her to the ground. She stood there quietly with her head bowed, adjusting the edges of her shawl, clutching them tightly together so they wouldn't slip and show her face. Her uncle lit a cigarette. Other men filed across the bridge and gathered round.

From here the bride was carried by the bridegroom's relatives. They spread a blanket on the ground and told her to lie down on it. Then they wrapped her up and tied her blanketed body to a pine-trunk. Four men then hoisted the pole from the ground, so it rested on their shoulders with the bride's body hanging down below. The procession set off again: the musicians first, drumming and dancing with increased bravado for the final approach to the village, then the bride and her bearers, and finally all the men from Lāmri and some of the men from Moharigāuṅ. Kāli and I walked beside the bride and her companions. We could hear her quietly sobbing underneath the blanket.

The bridegroom's house was soon aswarm with people – men, women, children, come to watch the celebrations, milling round, jostling one another on the confined space of the roof. In front of the house, on a patch of waste ground, the *Damāis* continued their dancing and drumming, now playing up to their noisily appreciative audience. Occasionally, as part of their act, they'd go up to someone, mesmerize them with their insidious drumming and unflinching gaze and, flashing their brilliant, irresistible smiles, proposition them for money. Sometimes they'd strike lucky and, in the spirit of generosity, a coin or two would be tossed their way. More often they'd be dismissed with a wave of the hand and a snort of indignation and mock-outrage.

Darkness was growing and little could be distinguished beyond the *Damāis'* white skirts and turbans, but the crowd still lingered, as did the bride and her two companions, sitting on their own, disassociated from the communal merriment. Inside the house a paraffin lamp had been lit. The bridegroom, wearing only his *dhoti*, was rubbing mustard oil into his face and chest and shaven head. When he had dressed in clean white clothes he sat down by the fire and the Brahman priest wrapped a new turban round his head and decorated his forehead with an intricate pattern of saffron and vermilion powders. Thus prepared, the young man was carried out of the house and into the stable below.

There was a small hearth in the stable and a fire had been lit.

Its flickering light cast deep shadows on the low beams and vertical wooden supports, giving the impression of infinite space, with one dimly lit recess unfolding continually on to the next. The cattle must have been in another stable, unless they were standing, or lying, motionless in a patch of total darkness. On the far side of the fire the bridegroom was sitting on a piece of cloth; next to him was the Brahman priest in a white *dhoti*, with his sacred thread, the symbol of his caste superiority, slung loosely over his bare chest and shoulders. In front of them, on the floor, was a petal-shaped oil-lamp and an ornate water container that represented Viśnu, Śiva, Ganeś and all of the gods in the orthodox Hindu pantheon. It had been decorated with red and white streamers and was embedded in a bronze bowl of unhusked barley.

Suddenly someone announced that the bride was coming, and two men rushed over and held up a length of cloth in front of the doorway. When they heard footsteps outside they lowered the cloth and the bride was carried in through the crowd. As she approached, the bridegroom threw a handful of rice grains at her and, with great cheers and hilarity, everyone delved into their pockets and did the same. The bride's bearer smiled good-naturedly and ducked his face behind his hand; but the bride, still shrouded in her blue and yellow shawls, sat motionless on his back, unperturbed by the pelting. When they'd made their way through the crowd the bride was set down on a seat of folded cloth beside her future husband, and her two female friends found a space to sit close by. The bridegroom's face was pale and expressionless. He didn't even turn his head towards his bride.

No one really understood the Sanskrit liturgy that the Brahman priest half-recited, half-read, in a hasty expressionless monotone, and people were talking among themselves and passing round *chillims* of tobacco, paying little attention. The crowd was made up entirely of men, with the exception of the bride, her two attendants, Kāli and myself, and three women standing at the back singing *māṅgals*, the traditional local songs that are sung on ritual occasions. They were mature women, unabashed by the strong male presence, and they sang with their heads raised. Their voices were powerful but light, carrying through the darkness and the thick smoky air.

As the couple performed each of the wedding rituals the crowd brightened up and attended. Everyone watched spellbound as the bride, having washed her hands, poured some water into a bowl and washed her future husband's feet. This done, she scooped up some of the water in the palm of her hand, shifted the shawl fractionally away from her mouth and tasted the water. Then the dirty water was taken away and a bowl of rice and curd was put down. The Brahman told the bride to eat from it first. She dipped her fingers in and put them briefly to her mouth. When the bowl was then passed to the bridegroom he too, wincing slightly, ate some rice. Everyone cheered and whooped as he did it knowing that, for the first and last time, he'd polluted himself by eating from the same plate as his wife.

The hilarity continued as a bowl of rice porridge was put down between the couple; when the Brahman priest gave the word, each of them grabbed a handful and tried to smear it on the other's face. Even though she couldn't really see because of her shawl, the bride immediately plastered a substantial glob across her husband's mouth; when he tried to retaliate she hid her veiled face behind her hands, while her two assistants reached across and splattered him on the chin and ear. Everyone wanted the bride to win, and I imagined her pleased and laughing to herself, thinking of her husband cleaning up his messy face.

Kāli was laughing too at this point; she seemed to have given up hiding behind her shawl and making herself invisible, and was craning her neck, like everyone else, to get a good view of the goings-on.

Again the audience's attention wandered while the priest's voice droned on. Then came the final ritual: the bridegroom, leaning forward, tied the end of his own white shawl, worn wrapped around his shoulders, on to the corners of his bride's blue and saffron ones. The bride was then helped to her feet and, with her two companions following behind, the two of them made their way three times round the sacred water-vessel with its red and white streamer decorations. After each circuit the crowd, unrestrainedly jubilant, shouted, 'Bihā bhayo!'

When they sat down again the priest put a rupee note over the lip of the water container and on it a little pile of red powder, called sindur. The groom dipped his finger into the sindur, leant towards his wife, who bowed her head while slightly adjusting the shawl, and painted a line of red along the parting of her hair. 'Bihā bhayo!' shouted the crowd – and the couple were married.

People stood up, stretching their legs and smiling, moving into clusters to talk. It was a happy occasion: the coming together of families and villages, the groundwork for new life, the affirmation of tradition and continuity.

The bride and bridegroom were picked up and carried by smiling vibrant bearers out of the stable and up the steps to the house. As they climbed on to the roof a gun was fired, announcing through the clear and frosty night that the wedding had taken place and they were now married. The bearers paused amid the women of the household who had gathered, waiting, at the threshold. Someone passed the bride a bowl of uncooked rice grains mixed with curd. She dipped her thumb into the mixture and, with guidance, printed three white marks on the cow-dung daubed above the doorway. The bridegroom, his young face beautiful and expressionless with its red and yellow markings, did the same and then the two were carried in.

Now, standing on her own two feet in her future home, the bride did what she knew she had to do – released the edges of her shawl so they slipped apart, and showed her face. The room fell silent as the members of her husband's family simply stared. For a moment she seemed as vulnerable as a butterfly, trapped when a collector's net claps down. But the moment passed – someone approached her, smiling, and marked a ṭikā between her eyes – the room filled up with voices, and the attention that had been focused on her alone diffused. Then, one by one, her father-in-law, mother-in-law, brothers- and sisters-in-law and all the members of her husband's lineage*, greeted her with ṭikās. Some of the older men and women dropped rupee coins into her own bowl of ṭikā mixture; she reciprocated by stooping down and planting ṭikās on their feet and, stooping lower, touching her forehead to their toes.

When everyone had welcomed her, she and her mother-in-law were coaxed into a corner and, weakly resisting, were urged to squat down on opposite sides of a great copper vat filled with unhusked rice. People gathered round, pressing in close to make sure they could see. The older woman was giggling shyly, masking her smile with her hand; the younger woman's face was calm, with that extreme self-consciousness that passes for serenity. Someone gave the word to start and the two women, leaning forward and rising slightly on their haunches, plunged their arms wrist-deep into the rice grains and swirled them round in search of something. From the sidelines people commented and shouted bantering encouragement, bursting into raucous laughter at their jibes. Then suddenly the bride let out a squeal of irrepressible delight. Grinning from ear to ear and showering a trail of rice grains on to the floor around her, she shot up her hand with a gleaming silver rupee. Everyone cheered, thrilled that it was she who'd found the coin and won; it was a good omen, a sign that she'd be strong and hard-working, that she'd bear fine sons and be an asset to her husband's family.

The revelling continued almost all through the night. The entire village, and all those who'd come from Moharigāuṅ, had to be feasted. The women of the household wove back and forth through the crowded room, fetching water for people to wash their hands and to drink, loading up plates, refilling them when

---

*A lineage is composed of all the male descendants of a common male ancestor. It is village-based, since men stay in their home villages on marriage. Women, on the other hand, marry 'out' – move to their husbands' homes, which are always in other villages. Sometimes the word lineage is used loosely to include the wives of related men and their young, unmarried daughters.

they were empty, taking the dishes outside to wash, then filling them up for other people. When almost everyone else had eaten Kāli and I sat down. Our plates were piled with *puris* and spicy fried potatoes, and when we'd finished these there was rice and *dāl*. Afterwards there was another helping of rice, this time mixed into a thick paste with a ladleful of cool and creamy curd. The bride and her friends ate in the quiet of the inner room and the women of the household, when they'd finished serving the food and eaten their own, joined them there. Only the men remained, drinking beer and talking into the early hours of the morning.

That night Kāli and I slept in the small grain-storage room next to the household shrine on the upper roof. At first it seemed bitterly cold, with only thin slats of wood and packed mud between us and the frosty night. But we nestled down under the rugs we'd been given and Kāli fell asleep almost immediately. Outside the celebrations were reaching their peak. Shouting and laughter rose from the stable where the *Damāi* drummers were cooking their chickens, the partial payment for the services. Men's muffled voices lilted drunkenly in the room below. I lay awake for a long time, staring out through a chink in the door, marvelling that the night could be so perfectly clear, the stars so bright.

When we set off in the morning we were given some *puris* and *lāḍus* to take home for Kalchu and Chola. As soon as we were outside the village, Kāli opened the birch-bark parcel and we helped ourselves to one of each, munching them happily as we walked along. Kāli was even more high-spirited than she had been on the way. We talked about the wedding and how beautiful the bride had looked with her face oiled and shining, her gold nose-ring and all her silver necklaces and bangles sparkling.

Then, quite out of the blue, as we were walking along, she suddenly announced that she herself was betrothed to be married, to a boy in Gorigāuṅ. Someone had come to discuss it with her father when she was only a few years old, and they'd clinched the arrangement by sharing a bottle of *raksi* and exchanging *ṭikās*. I asked what he was like – this future husband of hers – and she

169

laughed and made a face. 'Horrible. He's small as a girl and his skin's as black as dirt.'

As soon as we got back home the twins rushed over and grabbed hold of our legs, refusing to let go until we produced some *lāḍus*. Kāli's face looked crestfallen as she told them that we had none, that there'd been none to spare. At first they thought she was teasing and didn't believe her, but she persisted until tears of disappointment welled in their eyes. Then, with a huge grin, she produced the parcel and handed it over their heads to Chola who opened it and divided the *puris* and *lāḍus* into shares. While the twins were absorbed with the unfamiliar sweet taste of honey, Kāli told her parents about the wedding, adding that that was the kind of wedding she wanted, a proper Hindu wedding, a *kanyādān* wedding, with a Brahman priest and *Damāi* drummers, with thousands of people and masses of food.

When she'd finished, Kalchu started laughing and said there was no way he could afford a wedding like that. Apart from the payment for the *Damāi* drummers and the Brahman priest, and the cost of the food, the dowry she'd need would impoverish them: one cow, one sheep, one water container, one rug, one cooking pot, one plate, one bowl – one of just about everything they possessed. There'd be nothing left.

Three years later I heard that Kāli had had the kind of wedding she wanted. It was less lavish than the one we'd seen in Lāmri, but it was nevertheless a respectable Hindu wedding. The procession from Gorigāuṅ came to collect her one evening, and Kalchu's entire lineage helped to provide a feast for them and the whole of the village. All through the night there was singing and dancing, drinking and celebrating. In the morning before Kāli was taken away, Kalchu and Chola and the rest of the family had washed her feet in a bowl and drank from the water. Chola was crying and Kāli sobbed all the way to Gorigāuṅ.

MITINIS

THE DAY THAT JAKALI AND I WERE TO BECOME *MITINIS* SHE HAD prepared a feast. Her husband filled the bronze bowls with yellow barley beer and we sat around the fire sipping it, while she ground the salt and chilli and the spices and put the final touches to the meal. When everything was ready she filled up little pots with water and put them down for us to wash our hands, and before she served the meal she threw a few grains of rice into the fire for the household gods. There was always something special to eat at Jakali's – roasted amaranthus seeds, popped corn, green tomato chutney – and today, to celebrate, she produced some honey. It had been gathered in the autumn and stored away in a clay pot sealed with birch-bark and cow-dung. Inside, the honey was the colour of autumn leaves. Shards of wax and dead bees floated in it like the debris caught in a river eddy. That night, between us all, we devoured the entire pot.

'This is for life,' said Jakali. 'From now on my home will be your home and my children will be your children.' We marked each other's foreheads with red *ṭikās* and then Jakali went round, bending down to each person in the room including her baby who was sleeping by the fire, until we all had the same vermilion stain between our eyes. Then she gave the bowl of *ṭikā* mixture to her children and they played with it, daubing it on each other's hands and legs, duplicating the *ṭikās* on their foreheads until they spread from ear to ear like warpaint. After the *ṭikās* we gave each other gifts. Jakali went into the inner room and fetched a necklace intricately woven from many different-coloured tiny beads, and I gave her five red glass bracelets and a hair ornament that I'd bought in Kathmandu.

Jakali's children came to see me almost every day, making themselves at home whatever I was doing. Sometimes all five girls came trooping in together; sometimes just the younger ones would come, telling me proudly that Rām Chobār had gone to school – that she was the only girl in the village who went to

171

school – and that Bānchu was grazing the cows. Bānchu, the eldest, was beginning to take an interest in her appearance and always came with her face washed and oiled and her hair tidily plaited, showing me bits of jewellery and hairslides. The others never said a lot; they immersed themselves silently in my world, passing the time while their mother worked in the fields. One of them always brought the baby, wrapped in a shawl on her back, and sometimes they'd play with her, squeezing and tickling her, and feeding her imaginary mice to make her laugh. Jakali hadn't named the baby yet; she said she'd wait until she grew to be a girl and let the name suggest itself.

One autumn, when Jakali's husband had gone on a trading trip to the south, the two of us harvested her millet crop. We spent five days wading through the sea of grain, slicing heavy brown heads from their flimsy stalks with sickles and tossing them into baskets on our backs. Another time, in early summer, I helped her pick the purple *dāntelo* berries that she used for making oil. The *dāntelo* bushes grew wild around the village, between the fields and all along the river banks, and we wandered from one clump to another, scratching the backs of our hands on thorns as we rummaged for berries among the thick green foliage. When our baskets were full we took them to the stream and trod the mass of berries underwater so the fleshy pulp was washed away. Two of Jakali's daughters came rushing over when they saw what we were doing. She took off their clothes so they could play naked and they shrieked with delight as they flopped and splashed in the swirling purple water.

During the monsoon I didn't see Jakali for several weeks. She and her family had left the village, locking up their house with its beautiful carved window frame, and taking their cows, dogs and chickens to the monsoon settlements on the south-facing slopes of Jimale. Then one evening, when the rain had stopped for the first time since morning and the wind had swept the sky with watery blue and orange, she came to see me. I knew at once that there was something wrong; her face was strained and she was breathing hard as though she'd hurried. She sat down and carefully unwound the shawl that held the baby on her back. I gasped – the baby's head was covered in blisters; in places the film of skin had peeled away and the flesh beneath was red and angry.

'What happened?' I asked her. She told me that Rām Chobār had been looking after the baby while she and her husband were weeding. They were playing together and the baby had fallen into the fire. I looked from Jakali to the baby – both of them seemed in a state of shock, their eyes dry, their faces empty of expression, as though pain and tears had been temporarily suspended.

'We'll take her to the hospital in the morning,' I said, trying to sound encouraging. 'I'll come with you.'

But Jakali shook her head: the baby was too weak to survive the journey – it was dangerous to take her outside the village where evil spirits would enter her body through the open wound on her head. I tried to persuade her in every way I knew, but she was adamant. 'We'll take care of her together,' she said. 'Between us we can make her better.'

I put a pan of water on the fire to boil and fetched some iodine solution, cotton wool and lint, a jar of vaseline and a bandage from the small medicine box that I kept. The baby was lying across Jakali's lap, firmly clasped in the crook of her arm and half-heartedly sucking her breast. I waited for the water to cool. As soon as I touched the wound she cried and thrashed out, shocked at being hurt within the safe orbit of her mother's body.

The wound was already dirty where fluff, hair and bits of grit had lodged themselves in the soft raw flesh. It was impossible to get them all out, impossible to persevere against the baby's pain and distress. Jakali said it might be easier if she cleaned it up herself, so I passed her the cotton wool and the bowl of water, but the baby struggled almost as much. In the end all we could do was sluice the wound down, hoping that the iodine would prevent infection. When it had dried I covered it with a sheet of lint that I'd smeared with vaseline, and wound a bandage as best I could around the baby's head. Jakali left almost as soon as I'd finished, anxious to be back with her family on Jimale before it was dark.

Three days later I went, as I had said I would, to change the bandage. It was raining; the path up the hillside was steep and slippery, covered in places with tangled, waterlogged weeds, and the silence of the surrounding forest was broken only by the regular, ominous dripping of trees.

Jakali had told me that her shack was in the first clearing that you came to, only about half-way up the hillside, and I was glad when I left the dark forest and came out into the clear light of day. The upland wheat had already been harvested and cattle were grazing the stubble. I walked across the rough, stony ground towards the nearest of the three wooden huts. I knew that it was the right one when I saw one of Jakali's daughters rushing naked through the open doorway shouting, '*Mitini āmā ayo*'. Then she came running up to meet me.

Inside, a fire was burning in the central hearth. Jakali was sitting on the pine-needle floor, tapping out the dough for *rotis* between her palms and tossing the finished discs on to a heavy iron pan. The baby was lying across her lap, asleep. The bandage hadn't come undone, but it was very dirty and had slipped askew hanging down over one ear and half of an eye. Jakali smiled at me as she turned over a *roti* and, when it puffed up, removed it from the pan, standing it close to the embers to cook right through. She said that the baby seemed all right, but that she cried a lot, especially at night.

I didn't feel hungry but Jakali insisted, as she always did, that I eat. So Rām Chobār fetched me a pot of water to wash my hands and Jakali put two of the warm wheat *rotis* on to a plate and ladled out some curd from the wooden container. The swarm of flies that had been buzzing around aimlessly homed in immdiately on the food, and I waved them away as I ate.

Again the baby screamed and struggled when I went to touch her head. But this time Jakali was firm, talking soothingly, yet holding down her thrashing arms and legs. The dressing hadn't stuck, as I had feared it might, but underneath the wound was wet with blood and, in one small patch, with pus. I told Jakali that unless we took her to the hospital she might well die. But Jakali refused – she was too frightened for her.

I felt the baby's glands and they were slightly swollen, but she didn't seem to have a fever. So we boiled some water and washed the wound in iodine solution as before. When we'd finished the baby looked much happier. We'd washed her face as well and the skin on her cheeks was soft and tawny beneath the crisp white bandage. Jakali too seemed pleased and optimistic.

My own heart was weighted down with fear and sadness at their misplaced confidence. I told Jakali once again that I wasn't trained in medicine, that I didn't know how to save her baby. But when, moments later, I produced a bottle of ampicillin as a last resort, I merely reaffirmed her trust. Rām Chobār was delighted with the blue-and-yellow capsules, proud and thrilled that her little sister was to have this perfect, fail-safe medicine. I read the directions on the back of the bottle, tore up a piece of paper, and divided the contents of the capsules into four, parcelling each in a little twist of paper. We emptied one of them into some milk in a bowl and gave it to the baby there and then. She coughed a bit and swallowed. I told Jakali to give her one of these four times every day.

On the way back down through the forest I worried. Maybe I hadn't explained the instructions carefully enough – Jakali might give her too much or too little and either could be dangerous; maybe the baby was allergic to penicillin and Jakali wouldn't know to stop giving it to her if she developed a rash or had trouble breathing; maybe it would give her diarrhoea and, if she was weak anyway, she could lose her vital strength and die. I suddenly noticed that the light drizzle had become a teeming downpour. Raindrops hummed on the leaves and branches overhead and mingled with the pervasive whirring sound of crickets. The entire forest seemed to seethe with life.

When I returned to Jimale three days later, I was feeling calmer. Circumstances would have already taken their course and there was nothing to be done now but witness the results. On the way I met Rām Chobār in the forest picking wild raspberries with some other girls and she told me that her mother was out collecting pine-needles and would be back soon. She gave me a handful of raspberries to eat, and I savoured the fleshy orange pulp as I walked along. Soon afterwards I spotted Jakali on the path ahead, stooping under the weight of an enormous load of pine-needles. I called out to her and she waited for me, so we entered the clearing and approached the hut together.

The baby was lying face down on a shawl in the sun, kicking her feet in the air while her two sisters played with sticks in a patch of mud nearby. The bandage was even dirtier than it was before and it had slipped down to cover almost both her eyes; but she raised her head, peering out with difficulty, and smiled. Jakali put down her load of pine-needles and reached out her arms to pick her up. When she'd carried her inside she gave the baby her breast and after a while produced a little purse from her waistband, from which she took and carefully unravelled one of the paper twists of ampicillin.

This time the baby hardly cried at all when I started to unwind the bandage. Jakali said she thought she must be getting better: she almost never cried at night and sometimes, in the mornings, she'd clown around and make them laugh, as she always used to do. I unwrapped the last section of the bandage, and still apprehensive, eased off the lint dressing. Underneath, the baby's head was dry; a clean protective scab had formed over most of the wound and the patch of infection that I'd feared would spread had gone.

Jakali was thrilled. She squeezed the baby and hugged her, saying it was all right now, she was going to be all right. Feeling equally pleased and relieved, I dressed the wound again and bandaged it and gave Jakali some more of the paper twists of ampicillin.

The following day Jakali and her family abandoned their settlement on Jimale and moved back down to the village. They arrived in the evening, driving the cows, with the dogs following behind, the chickens packed up in one basket, and blankets and cooking pots crammed into another.

That autumn we saw a lot of one another. The baby's head slowly got better. Gradually the scab peeled off and was replaced by a layer of delicate pinkish skin. Jakali was worried that the hair would never grow, that she'd always be bald where the burn had been. But in time one or two straggly tufts pushed through. She kept the bandage on for a long time: at first because she was afraid of the baby scratching the itchy scab and then later because, until the wound was perfectly healed, she was frightened of evil spirits.

When Jakali came to see me now she nearly always brought a little gift – some eggs or potatoes, a plateful of maize flour – and at festivals and other special occasions she always invited me to her house to eat. Once her brother came to visit them from Moharigāuṅ and she killed a chicken for him. Her brother was a very worldly man – he'd travelled and worked in India and for several years had had a government job in Jumla. Jakali's children loved him because he told them about his adventures, and every so often he'd break off a conversation with their father to indulge and play with them.

Then, several days afterwards, she invited me for another meal. It was the night before her husband was to go on his annual trading trip to the southern border. All evening people dropped in to say goodbye. Jakali poured out bowls of beer and *raksi* for them and the night dissolved into laughter and stories until, quite unexpectedly, it was dawn.

After he'd gone I helped Jakali make some beer that would ferment, to be ready for his return in three weeks time. We sat on the roof to avoid the smoke in the house while the vat of barley boiled and boiled. Occasionally one or other of us would go inside to check that it hadn't boiled dry and to add some more wood to the fire. When at last it was soft Jakali tipped it on to the newly-plastered floor to let it cool. We crumbled in the yeast and then crammed it all back into the vat, covering it over with a sheet of birch-bark. After three days the fermentation had begun and we transferred it into a clay jar which Jakali sealed with cow-dung. Every day she put the jar out in the warmth of the sun; every night she brought it in.

One evening we were sitting by Jakali's fire, carding wool. Bānchu and Rām Chobār were out somewhere and the three younger girls were asleep. We'd been silent for some time, concentrating on the wool, when Jakali suddenly said that her husband was going to take a second wife.

'Why?' I asked, shocked.

Jakali didn't lift her eyes from the matted greasy wool that she was deftly teasing into a soft white froth. She said that she'd only given him daughters and he wanted a son.

I thought for a minute about what she was saying. I knew that some people who didn't have sons married their daughters at home rather than sending them to live in their husband's villages. 'Couldn't Bānchu's husband come and live here with you after they're married?' I asked. 'That way there'd be somebody to help with the land and to look after you both when you're old.'

'My husband's far too proud for that,' she said. 'And anyway, only a real son who's flesh and blood can perform his funeral rites.'

Jakali had been married before – an arranged marriage to a man in Chaura. When she met her present husband they'd fallen in love; he'd paid adultery money to her first husband and she'd run away to live with him. I could tell from her voice and the sadness in her face that she loved him still. The real tragedy, however, was that, in her first marriage, she'd given birth to two sons, but their father had kept them both. Now, she wasn't sure she could conceive again.

'What are you going to do?' I asked, concerned for her.

'Learn to live with her, I suppose.' A few moments passed and she looked up from her cloud of wool. 'Sometimes we'll laugh and sometimes we'll cry.'

MINA

WHEN MINA MARRIED ŚAŃKAR SHE DIDN'T HAVE AN ORTHODOX
Hindu wedding like the one that Kāli was to have. She too was
betrothed to be married when she was a little girl. Then when
she became a woman, Śaṅkar and one or two other men arrived
in Gorigāuṅ with the traditional five hundred *puris* for her family.
Śaṅkar drew the line of *sindur* in her hair, her family washed her
feet, and she was taken away. No doubt there was some small
celebration – with *puris* and beer – but there was no question of
the entire village being feasted. It was the kind of wedding most
people had: cheap, informal, practical.

Three years later Mina still felt an outsider in her husband's
family. She and Śaṅkar rarely spoke to one another, or even
looked at one another and, in public at least, showed no affection
at all. Kalchu too ignored her most of the time. When he did
address her she averted her eyes and replied in a whisper. Chola
was less reserved with her – the two women worked together
almost every day; but if a job wasn't done properly it was
invariably Mina's fault for being lazy or going off enjoying herself
when she was needed at home. Only the younger children treated
her with warmth and affection: to Kāli Mina was like an elder
sister – someone to talk to and play at being a woman with. For
the twins she was a reassuring female presence to run and cling
to when their mother wasn't there.

Whenever possible Mina spent her time outside the house. In
the mornings as soon as she was up she'd go and fetch the water.
Usually she'd linger for a while at the stream, washing her face,
talking to other women, smoking a *chillim*, before she filled the
copper container and carried it home. She liked going on trips to
the forest with other women, collecting firewood or pine-needles;
and in late summer, going to the steep mountain slopes and
gathering grass to feed the cattle in winter. On those days she left
the house at dawn, stuffing a couple of *roṭis* into her waistband,
and didn't return until the last streaks of sunset were fading to

grey. As long as she returned with her load by nightfall no questions were asked; she was not accountable for the hours spent lying in the grass, talking and laughing.

When she returned on evenings like that, and sat quietly eating her meal while the rest of the family chattered and scrabbled around her, she seemed to know something that none of the others could know. There was a strength in her silence, and pride. Afterwards, she'd gather up the dirty dishes and take them outside to wash. As she squatted in the darkness, scrubbing out pans with charcoal and ash, her secret stayed with her, sure as an amulet.

Often, exasperated by the constraints of her family gathering – by not being able to talk or even smoke when her father-in-law was there – she'd come and spend the evening with me. She always talked quietly, afraid that they'd know she was there and think it a betrayal. But her anger was unmistakable: an outpouring of grievances and complaints. Sometimes I'd commiserate with her, as she crammed tobacco into her *chillim* and rummaged furiously in the fire for an ember to light it. But often, by the time we'd engulfed ourselves in clouds of tobacco smoke, she'd soften and we'd both be laughing.

At festivals Mina went home to her natal family, her *māiti* in Gorigāun. She loved those times: of being spoilt by her parents; of not having to do any work other than fetching the water and pounding the rice; of being surrounded by people she knew and grew up with – her younger brothers and sisters, her uncles and aunts and cousins and her grandmother, an old woman now, who was blind and lived with her parents. All of them made a fuss of her and pressed her to tell them her gossip.

On several occasions Mina didn't come back with the other women whose *māitis* were in Gorigāun. Once, days passed and there was still no sign of her. Chola was furious; furious at having to cover for her, at all the extra work she was having to do. She stormed around the house ranting about Mina; complaining that they couldn't sow the wheat on Jimale until she was back and it was already getting late; that because of her, she'd have to spend all night at the watermill. The day was only so long and she couldn't do everything – she was a selfish bitch, a useless lazy slut.

Mina turned up early in the morning of the ninth day. She looked very sheepish as she opened the door and took a few steps into the room where everyone was sitting, eating. She didn't say a word – no apology, no excuses – just stood there staring at the ground, waiting for whatever had to happen. Surprisingly no one raised their voice. Chola muttered a few words under her breath while she ladled out some maize porridge and passed it to her. Kalchu and Śaṅkar said nothing, simply carried on eating.

Late that evening, when they'd all come back from the fields, Mina came to sit with me. We smoked my cigarettes, although she always said she preferred her own clay *chillim* with its dry home-grown tobacco. She told me she hadn't wanted to come back at all; every day she'd dreaded it more. Her father tried to persuade her, saying how good and kind Kalchu and Chola were, what a good family it was, and how, in the end, she'd be happy to be here. She didn't want to upset him, but as the days went by it became impossible. In the end he insisted.

Mina's face looked very young, and in the dim light of the fire, very beautiful. As she held the cigarette to her mouth, the skin on her cheeks looked soft as dough beside her cracked, work-blackened hands. She was wearing a blue-and-orange bead necklace that she'd woven while she was away, and a new crossover jacket had replaced her patched and faded one. On an impulse I asked if she was in love with someone else. But she said that no, she'd stay with Śaṅkar. She smiled her inscrutable smile: he might be stupid and ugly but at least he never beat her.

Not long after that I was woken in the night by a door being screeched open and the sound of footsteps and voices whispering urgently on the roof. I looked out. There was no moon and at first it seemed utterly dark. Then two figures approached making their way towards the back steps. One of them was bent over, clutching her stomach as though she was in pain. The other had her arm around her and was helping her along. Both of them wore loose dark clothes – skirts with blankets draped around their heads and shoulders – and it took me some time to recognize them as Mina and Chola.

I didn't follow them or say anything at the time because I sensed a complicity between the two and was afraid I'd be intruding. But in the morning I asked Chola what the commotion had been about. She told me that Mina had started to miscarry in the night and that she'd taken her down to the stable so she wouldn't pollute the house.

Later that day, when everyone else was out in the fields, Mina came to talk to me. She stood outside the open door and refused to come inside. She was looking terrible: her face was pinched and ashen, and her young body had somehow withered overnight. She said she was still in pain, still bleeding. When I asked her if there was anything I could do, she said she'd like some maize flour fried in oil: that would stem the bleeding. So I made a fire and prepared it for her. Afterwards we sat on the roof in the sun for a while. I offered her a cigarette and she held out her cupped hands like an Untouchable and motioned for me to drop it into them, afraid that her fingers on one end of it would pollute my own on the other end.

Mina stayed in the stable for nine days, coming outside only occasionally: to warm herself in the sun; when she needed to relieve herself; and – on the first morning, when it was still half-dark and she couldn't be seen – to take her aborted foetus down to the river and throw it away. In the evenings she made herself a small fire. Chola brought food down to her and occasionally she or Kāli and the twins would sit and talk to her for a while before she wrapped herself up in her blankets and lay down for the night.

On the morning of the tenth day Mina went down to the stream to wash. It was barely dawn when she arrived and there was just enough light reflected off the water for her to gather some twigs and light a fire on the bank. When the twigs were burning she surrounded them with three big stones and set a pan of water on top to boil. Sheltered from the wind, the flames grew stronger and Mina squatted down raising her palms to their warmth. While she was waiting for the water to heat she filled a *chillim* and smoked it contentedly. Occasionally she'd add some more twigs or a larger piece of wood to the fire, and when a sudden draught dampened the flame, stirring the smoke into turmoil, she'd put her cheek to the ground and blow.

Mina washed everything: the tattered skirt that she'd printed herself with bright red and green vegetable dye, though it was now universally brown; her older patched jacket; her white waist-band; her shawl; the blankets she'd slept in. She refilled the pan again and again, but in the frosty air the water was slow to heat. Most of the time she used cold water, soaking the clothes, mixing them with white wood ash that she'd brought in a separate bowl, pummelling them with a wooden board, and finally rinsing the loosened dirt in the stream.

By the time she'd started washing her hair and body, a steady flow of people were coming to the stream, filling their water containers, washing their faces and hands. One other woman had brought a basket of clothes to wash and was lighting a fire close to Mina's – ending the four-day pollution of her menses.

When Mina got back to the house the sun had risen and the sky was a fathomless blue. Chola was squatting down smearing mud and cow-dung solution on to the floor in circular movements, cleansing the house. When she saw Mina she reached for a little bronze pot of cow's urine that she'd collected earlier. Dipping her fingers into the clear yellowish liquid, she sprinkled some into the room and some over Mina. Then she passed the container to Mina who drank a drop or two, and was finally purified.

Gradually Mina recovered from her miscarriage, and when she moved up to Jimale in the monsoon her body finally regained its fullness and her face its childlike clarity. It was a season of little work; a season when the crops grew and ripened in the warmth and rain and had only to be weeded. Mina rested. She picked raspberries and strawberries, gathered woodland mushrooms, drank the milk and curd that, for those few months, flowed in abundance.

It must have been around this time that she conceived again, because her baby was born in the spring. I don't know when she realised she was pregnant, or was certain, but she didn't tell me until there was only one month left to go – and I never suspected it. All through the autumn and winter she worked as hard as she normally would: harvesting the crops and bringing them in; gathering firewood, shifting basketloads of *mal* from the stable to the paddy fields. I didn't even notice her body change – all the women wore waistbands so thick, so pouched out with *chillims* and tobacco and bits and pieces, it was impossible to tell if they were pregnant or not. Nor did I wonder why she didn't sleep in the stable for four days every month – some women did, some didn't.

Her labour began in the night. Chola filled a basket with split firewood, sticks of *jharo* for lighting and enough blankets to keep the two of them warm, and helped her down to the stable. Mina told me afterwards that she was glad the baby had come in the night: the darkness was intimate and private. If she and Chola had had to make their way back from the fields in the daytime when the pain had already begun, everyone would have known. It would have been shameful.

I don't know how long the two of them were down there – this time I didn't wake – but I imagine it was most of the night: waiting, enduring the pain. Mina didn't remember it clearly. She remembered drifting into sleep, then waking to the cows' creaking limbs and soft grunts, each time expecting it to be dawn, then realising it wasn't the dawn she was waiting for. She remembered Chola's presence – a vague form moving about, adding wood to the fire and rearranging the logs, then, when the pains intensified, looming above her, touching, holding, adjusting her body.

When Kalchu heard that Mina's baby was a boy he was beside himself with happiness: the first-born son of his own first-born son – his only grandchild. He and Śaṅkar took the gun from its place in the rafters and, standing on the upper roof, pointed it high into the clear sky and fired, two, three, four, five, and six times. Then he went into the house and rummaged around looking for a bottle of *raksi*. He was smiling to himself, glowing with the knowledge of his grandson, and when he removed the birch-bark bung and poured out two bowls of the clear, strong-smelling liqueur, his smile radiated into sheer exuberant laughter.

Soon afterwards the *Damāi* drummers arrived, alerted by the gunfire, and installed themselves on the roof, pounding out the celebratory rhythm for a newborn son. For six days they would come, morning and evening, fanfaring the baby's passage into the world, and for six days Kalchu and Chola would give them their meals in partial payment. Later they'd be joined by young girls and boys dancing and singing traditional birth-songs on the roof beside them. Inside the house Kalchu had opened another bottle of *raksi*, and another, and he and Śaṅkar were getting slowly tipsy as friends and relatives came trooping by to celebrate.

Mina's baby was strong and healthy and so dark-skinned, even from birth, that Nara and the twins teased her and affectionately called it the *Ḍum**. Kāli doted on him; she spent most of the time in the stable, holding him, hugging him, cuddling him and bouncing him around when he started to cry. Mina too, as she regained her strength, was contented. She loved all the attention that was lavished on her: the sounds of drumming and singing on the roof above; the special food she was given to eat – Kalchu had killed a chicken for her, and her father, when he heard the news, had sent another one over from Gorigāuṅ.

Mina didn't leave the stable much for the first few days of the baby's life. In a way she was glad of the enforced isolation that was made necessary because of her pollution. But as soon as she felt strong enough – the second night after the birth – she wrapped the placenta in her blood-stained skirt and took the bundle down

*Many *Ḍum* families migrated to the area from the south, and their skin is often darker than other Nepalis'.

to the river. She buried it in the soft ground on the bank and went to the water to wash. For two days she didn't feed the baby herself, thinking that the first milk was bad for him, and Chola found a wet-nurse, a woman whose own baby was partially weaned. Mina was afraid that she wouldn't be able to feed him herself, that she'd be dry, so when she did give him her breast, and after one or two attempts the milk began to flow, she was pleased and relieved: he'd be a round plump baby and, in time, would grow into a robust little boy.

On the sixth day Mina's pollution ended and she went to the river, lit a fire and washed. When she'd sprinkled herself with cow's urine and touched some to her lips, she wrapped the baby in a clean shawl, hoisted him gently on to her back, and for the first time, carried him out of the stable and up the steps to the house. The floor had been freshly plastered and there were a lot of people sitting around the fire, waiting to see the baby, to greet him, and welcome him into the family. Kalchu's brother gave him a bracelet – a string of blue-and-white beads with a single silver coin, that all his own sons had worn to protect them when they were babies – and Śaṅkar tied it carefully on to his wrist. Mina's father and brother had come from Gorigāuṅ, and Jakali and two other women were singing *māṅgals* to commemorate this very special occasion.

Kalchu apologized that he hadn't killed a goat – they were still away in the south. But there were *puris* and rice, *dāl*, wild greens and beer, and everyone seemed happy. Even the baby bore up to the attention; to being passed from Śaṅkar to Kalchu, to Kāli – whom he was already beginning to know – and back again. Eventually he started to cry and Mina picked him up and took him out of the room into the sunshine.

CHOLA

THE POTATO HARVEST SEEMED TO LAST FOREVER: ONE SMALL
patch of land after another; row upon row of withered plants to
be dug up, the earth beneath crumbled and sifted. Kalchu went
first with the plough, steering the bulls down each line, talking
to them, whooping and whistling when they slackened, swishing
his long willow twig so it cracked on to their bony rumps and
jolted them back into action. Chola, Mina, the children and I
followed behind, bending over, rummaging through the loosened
earth and tossing the pallid potatoes into small cylindrical baskets.

The early mornings at that time of year were cold; Kalchu had
to lean all his weight on the wooden plough, forcing it into the
frosty earth, and Kāli and Nara complained that their hands were
stiff and aching. Every so often they'd straighten up and blow on
them or rub them together to bring the blood-flow back to their
fingers. But if we hadn't gathered all the potatoes from one row
before Kalchu turned and began ploughing the next, Chola would
shout at them to stop messing about: if they worked a bit harder
their hands might warm up.

As the sun rose, its warmth settled first on our stooped-over
backs, then seeped gradually through to our hands and our feet.
By midday the light was so bright it was dazzling. Kalchu, the
bulls and the line of crouching bodies, drained of their colour and
substance, became silhouettes against the white glare of the earth.
Dust rose in the wake of the plough, coating our faces, clinging
to our hair and eyelashes. The twins, tired of playing on their
own, of digging for stray potatoes in furrows we'd long since
abandoned, became restless and bored, tugging at Chola's skirt
and clamouring for food. When Chola stood up to placate them
she felt suddenly dizzy. She leant forward, resting her head in her
hands with the palms cupping her cheekbones and the muddy
fingers shading her eyes.

When she looked up Kāli, who was next in line along the
furrow, had stopped working and was staring at her, concerned.

She dropped the potato she was holding into the basket at her feet and made her way back through the churned-up soil. Chola said she was all right now – the dizziness had passed. When she'd reassured Kāli, she told her to go and gather a basketload of dry sticks so they could light a fire and cook some potatoes: she was probably just weak with hunger.

Not long afterwards blue smoke gusted horizontally through the dust and sunlight. Kalchu called out to the bulls to stop, and unhitched them from the plough, letting them wander off in search of grass among the dry earth and shrivelled plants. Chola, Mina and I finished the furrow we'd been working on, emptied our small baskets into the bigger ones at the edge of the plot, and joined the others by the fire.

Kāli had chosen the biggest potatoes to roast – great bulbous globes. Their skins, still covered in earth, were thick and black, charred by the flames, and we peeled them, burning our fingers in our haste to get to the crumbling, yellowish flesh. Most of them were hardly cooked in the centre and Chola teased Kāli for her greediness, saying that potatoes that size wouldn't be properly cooked before nightfall. But they tasted good, washed down with the cold water that Mina had fetched from the river; and when they were finished we rummaged through the fire with sticks, searching for remaining ones that were burnt so black they were hidden in the embers.

We didn't go back to work straight away. Kalchu went to empty the potatoes we'd gathered into the pit where they were stored for the winter, so we sat and smoked a *chillim*, waiting for him to come back and rehitch the bulls. Chola said her body was aching from bending down all morning, and Lāla Bahādur, still not satisfied after the food, was whinging for her attention. In exasperation she lifted her jacket and pulled out her breast, and he sat on her lap while she smoothed his pale brown hair, bristled into spikes and knots from the dust. For a while he seemed contented, his eyes like still pools amid the dirt and streaks of black from the burnt potato skins. But he was too restless to be a baby for long. Soon he scrambled to his feet, and sniffing a trail of thick snot back into his nostril, wandered off to join the others. Cursing him, Chola put away her breast.

In the hours that followed no one talked much. We fell into the rhythm of the work, losing ourselves in a subterranean world where nothing existed beyond the texture of the soil, the feel of the potatoes: big ones that filled the hand; little ones that clustered round the tangled roots like pebbles caught in river-weed. And in the background, as though from some distant place, we dimly heard the drone of Kalchu's voice and the creaking of the plough as it rumbled back and forth: into the sun, away from the sun.

We stopped working when the sun finally disappeared altogether, dropping behind the mountain and casting the entire valley in shadow. Suddenly it felt bitterly cold, with an icy northerly wind that the sun's warmth had disguised.

I didn't work on the potato harvest every day. Most of the time I stayed at home, reading and writing. On one such day Chola came back from the fields early so she could press some oil to fry the *puris* for Sigarup's departure to Aula in a few days' time. She fetched the paste that she'd made from roasted hemp seeds, and the little wooden gully on which she pressed it, and knelt down, ready to begin. When I went on to the roof to join her she said, 'Sister, everything's so easy for you. You have oil and ghee; you have spices of every kind; you eat meat and eggs and honey and rice as often as you like; you have medicine, contraceptives, nice clothes, soap to wash with; you don't have to work in the fields all day – you can just sit at home, reading and writing ... '

She'd said all this to me before, several times, and now I acknowledged the truth – and half-truth – of it once again. She leant down with all her weight, forcing her knuckles into the paste, then folding it over and forcing her knuckles in again so the skin showed white across her fists. I watched as the oil seeped out and trickled down the wooden gully, falling drop by drop into the small bowl at the bottom and spreading slowly out across its surface.

The next time I went to Jumla Bazaar I bought some meat and invited the whole family – Kalchu, Chola, their seven children and Mina – to eat with me. It took me most of the day to prepare the food, battling with the heat of the fire and the smoke, borrowing plates and bowls and large cooking pots and pans from Chola. Apart from the meat there was yellow lentil *dāl*, spicy potatoes, rice, fresh green chillies that I'd bought in the Bazaar and a couple of bottles of *raksi*.

When it was ready Chola came in first, pushing open the door very gingerly, turning and whispering – making sure the others were coming close behind – then taking Lāla Bahādur by the hand and almost tiptoeing inside. Although she came to see me often, today she acted like a guilty child living out some long-dreamt-up, forbidden fantasy. Slowly, savouring the moments, she sat down by the fire. Her eyes were shining with anticipation and her own particular sense of fun and mischief as she gazed around, taking in all my possessions as though she was seeing them for the first time: commenting on the books, the torch, the camera, the plastic containers that she'd always coveted; saying how bright and clean everything looked in the steady light of the paraffin lamp.

I poured out the bowls of *raksi*: one for Kalchu, one for Śankar, Sigarup, Mina, Chola, myself. Mina refused hers when I passed it to her, shuffling it back across the floor and looking embarrassed, as though she wished I hadn't offered. Chola exchanged glances with Kalchu, implying that I'd made some kind of social blunder, offering alcohol to women when men were there. She too refused hers; then suddenly, her eyes alight, she changed her mind, deciding that she would indulge herself: she'd share it with the children.

I heaped up the plates and passed them round, waiting until everyone else had finished before eating my meal, watching their progress, ladling out more rice, more *dāl*, more meat as each plate was emptied and emptied again. I was glad that, for once, it was not Chola who ate the remains in the pans when everyone else had finished; glad to see her passing her plate for more, tearing the last shred of meat from one bone after another, smacking her lips as she bit into a green chilli and the fresh juice seared through her mouth, tingling and burning.

As each person finished they went out on to the roof to wash their hands and Kalchu told Mina to clear up the plates and dishes and take them outside to wash. The more I objected, the more insistent he became. In the end I followed her out and told her not to bother, she was a guest tonight. But she said she preferred being outside to sitting in there with her parents-in-law; she could smoke out here, and afterwards it would be a good excuse to slip away to someone else's house.

I refilled the bowls of *raksi*, laughing as Lāla Bahādur let go of Chola's breast and seized her bowl instead. 'Sister,' said Chola, ignoring him, 'is it really true that in your country it's early morning now – that when it's night-time here it's daytime in America?'

'That's right,' I said. I'd given up trying to explain that I wasn't American and that while America was approximately ten hours behind Nepal, England was somewhere in between.

'How can that be possible?' she pondered, smiling through her confusion at the total absurdity of it.

My Nepāli didn't rise to an explanation of that so Kalchu took over. With great animation he began talking and gesticulating, describing a circle above his head with his arms, then drawing on the mud floor with a piece of wood, mentioning the sun, the moon, the earth, the sky and the stars.

I couldn't understand what he was saying – nor, I think, could Chola, because after a minute or two she changed the subject, drowning him out. 'And sister,' she said, looking thoughtful, 'is it really true that each one of your cows yields thirty *mānās* of milk every day ... and that your fish grow as long as your arm?'

'Some do,' I said. 'Some grow even bigger. There are big fish and there are little fish. Some are only half the size of yours.' I tried to explain the difference between marine fish and river fish; between the ocean and a river.

'Wha, wha, wha!' she said, shaking her head, impressed but sceptical.

'She's never even seen a car, never tasted a banana,' said Sigarup, her second-eldest son, who'd travelled south many times, trading and grazing the sheep. 'She's never been outside this valley – never even been to Jumla!'

Several weeks went by. The potato harvest ended; Kalchu covered the underground storage pits with earth and a thick layer of thorn bushes to stop wild boar and other foragers digging down and raiding them. Sigarup left for Aula with the sheep. The first snow fell.

One evening we were all sitting in the warmth by the fire when Chola suddenly leaned forward, resting her head in her hands and said she was feeling terribly dizzy. Seconds later her whole body started shaking, gently at first, then convulsively. When she looked up her eyes were flickering like butterflies and she had to gasp for breath as though her throat had tightened up and blocked. 'Aha, aha, aha' – the sound came out in clipped, rhythmic grunts. Chola was possessed.

The sight of her, so transformed, both shocked and frightened me. I'd seen her possessed before, but that had been at one of the big full-moon festivals when any number of people had suddenly sprung to their feet, dancing and cavorting, possessed by one or other god. Then, she'd been wearing a garland of marigolds and her face had been calm and radiant as she danced around, dispensing smiles like silver coins among the audience. Now she looked bad-tempered, hostile. She said something to Kalchu in a strange voice that I didn't understand and he disappeared to fetch a plate of rice-grains. When he put it down in front of her she stirred the rice-grains round for a minute and then went over to Lāla Bahādur who'd been crying and sulking most of the day. Muttering angrily, she waved a handful of the rice-grains three times round his head, pushed open the door, went to the edge of the roof, and flung the rice-grains into the air. Something had been bedevilling the child – now it was gone.

The following day Chola had a pain in her stomach and vomited several times. Instead of getting better as the day progressed the pain got worse. By evening it was intense and persistent, gradually spreading from her stomach to her chest and heart. Kalchu was worried; he told the *dhāmi* that he needed to call the gods to the shrine that night.

For a long time the drums rumbled and the great bell clanged but the gods wouldn't come. Then, eventually, the *dhāmi* began shaking. 'Aha, aha, aha.' As soon as the clamour of the bell and the drums had died down and the *dhāmi* had taken off his *topi* and loosened his hair, Kalchu put the questions he had come to ask: which god was possessing his wife – and why was she ill?

The god said he didn't know which of the other gods it was. He couldn't even be sure which village he came from, although it was likely, because he wouldn't identify himself, that he came from somewhere far away, like Rini or Padmāra. Some of the men in the shrine made suggestions and, for a while, everyone discussed the possibilities. Then the god said, 'But one thing is clear. Your wife is ill because when that god chose her – when that god came to her – her body wasn't fit for him.'

Again the men in the shrine became animated, talking to the god and among themselves. I didn't understand the conversation: partly because it was so fast and heated, and partly because the *dhāmi*'s voice – the god's voice – and the words he used were strange and new to me. Then, suddenly, the shrine fell silent and I realized everyone was staring at me as though expecting some response. I looked at Kalchu who was sitting beside me, and he explained, 'The god has asked you if she has eaten any food that you have cooked while you were menstruating.'

'No,' I muttered.

So it wasn't that. The discussion continued and after a while there was silence again. Kalchu leaned over to me. 'Sister,' he said, 'you have to pay a fine of five rupees to the shrine. The god has made her ill because, when he came to her, her body was polluted from eating foreigners' food. The money is a kind of penance – an apology to both of them.'

I left the men talking in the shrine, found my shoes which I'd taken off outside the door, and went to the house to fetch the money.

After that I didn't know how to respond to Chola. She felt better almost immediately and didn't seem to bear me any malice or resentment. But I felt unhappy; Kalchu too was a bit on edge. So one evening I sat and talked to him about it. He said it wasn't just my food that Chola couldn't eat; if the god was going to come to her regularly, then she'd be a *dhamini*, a female *dhāmi* – and as with any *dhāmi*, there were certain impure foods that she couldn't eat: chicken, eggs, *raksi*, beer. I nodded, understanding, wondering whether Chola had it in her to turn down chicken meat that was offered her; doubting it.

I never saw Chola possessed again, although I did see her refusing chicken meat. Gradually, however, when it seemed as though the god had abandoned her, she reverted to her former ways, drinking, at first, weak beer with water added, and taking little nibbles of chicken from the children's plates.

The next time I cooked for the whole family, almost a year later, there was no question of Chola being excluded. She was as eager as a child: loving the occasion and relishing the food.

SAUNI

KĀLI'S SISTER, SAUNI, CAME HOME FROM HER HUSBAND'S VILLAGE
the day before the rice transplanting was due to start. She'd been
married for nearly two years, but after less than one her husband
had left for the south, and although his family had tried to contact
him in every way that they knew, nothing had been heard of him
since. At the time Sauni had been too young and beautiful, too
full of the possibilities of happiness to tolerate the bleakness of her
abandonment and, during the long months of his absence, she'd
fallen in love with someone else. At first their love had been as
secret as spring flowers under snow, but as time had taken its
course, her father-in-law had inevitably heard. Angry and
outraged, he'd insisted that, although his son had been gone for
a long time, he'd be back; that, like it or not, Sauni was a married
woman – his own daughter-in-law – and if she ran away to her
lover in Chaura, he'd have to pay them five thousand rupees –
the price of her adultery.

Most of the time Sauni believed that, one day, her lover and
his family would raise the money and she'd be free to go and live
with him. But in the mean time, life with her husband's family
was barely tolerable. Either they were openly hostile, or they
spurned her with silent disapproval. At festivals, and at times like
this – the rice transplanting – when she came home to her *māiti*
to celebrate or to help with the agricultural work, she became a
different woman. No longer intimidated and bowed down with
shame, she laughed and relaxed, blossoming in the certainty that,
for these few days, away from the ubiquitous gaze of her husband's
village, she'd be with her lover again.

The paddy seeds for planting had been set aside to soak two
months ago on the day of the new moon in *Chait*. After three days
in water they'd been spread in the sun to dry and then returned
to covered containers to sprout in the darkness. When white buds
of shoots began to emerge, Kalchu had taken the seeds and
scattered them broadcast on one of his fields. Then, during the

time that it took for the roots to establish and the slender green leaves to appear, he'd worked on preparing the rest of his rice-land: irrigation channels had been undammed so that water from the river had flooded through; the swamped fields had been ploughed and reploughed, churning water, soil and *mal* into a smooth wet sludge; mud banks between rough terraces had been built up and repaired, preventing the surface water from seeping away and draining down to the level below.

On the morning of Sauni's return, everyone was preparing for the following day: Kalchu, Sigarup and Śankar had gone to the paddy fields to uproot the young seedlings and bundle them into clumps tied with a single stem, ready to be transplanted. Kāli, Mina, Sauni and I went down to the stream to wash our hair. It was a beautiful mid-June day, clear and hot, and the water, before the monsoon rains and after the tide of melted snow from the mountains, was warm enough to make washing a pleasure. We used my shampoo brought from the city, instead of the usual mud, and the three of them laughed and shrieked with delight as the smooth white foam enveloped their heads and wafted away when they flicked it into the wind.

Afterwards we sat on the roof in the sun and Sauni lay back against Kāli's shins as she bent over her, oiling and combing her hair, parting it into little squares, then plaiting each square into a thin braid that crept up from her temples to join the main plait at the back of her head. When the plait reached the nape of her neck, Kāli started to weave in a black cotton braid with a red tassel at the end. Sauni's hair was thin and straggly and only shoulder length, but the end result, as Kāli secured the braid at the bottom, was of luxuriant, heavy tresses reaching right down below her waist. Kāli swished the red tassel over her sister's shoulder – a final flourish to say she'd finished – and Sauni sat up, feeling the plait with her hand. She asked to borrow my pocket-miror and looked at herself for several minutes, holding the mirror close at first, scrutinizing the neatness of the plaiting, then further away to take in the general effect of her face and hair, her silver and coral necklaces, the metal hairslides that she'd fixed in a row down the front edge of her jacket.

'You're beautiful,' said Kāli, half with reverence, half with sarcasm. Sauni made as if to lash out, embarrassed by her comment. But she didn't need the mirror, and she didn't need her sister's compliments, to tell her she was beautiful. Although she wasn't vain, everything about her – the way she wore her clothes and jewellery, the way she walked and held herself, her sudden radiant bursts of heartfelt laughter – bespoke an inner knowledge of her beauty.

We weren't ready to leave for the paddy fields until the sun had rolled high into the open sky. Kalchu and the boys had left much earlier, but it had taken time for Chola to prepare the food to take, for us all to dress in our best clothes, for Sauni and Mina to wash and polish their silver jewellery with ash and to recover from the debilitating fits of giggles that overcame them every time they attempted to paint the traditional blue spots and stripes on each other's faces, then on Kāli's and on mine. We were just about ready when Kāli delighted us all by producing a basketful of rhododendron flowers – the very last ones, she said, that she'd had to climb high up the hillside to find – and with a display of self-conscious flamboyance, we slipped the heavy crimson blossoms into our plaits and behind our ears.

Walking the half-mile or so to the paddy fields we were a party of about ten women, mostly with children: babies carried in shawls on backs; toddlers being trailed along by the hand; young girls and boys running excitedly ahead, investigating everything that caught their eyes along the path. Each year most women worked on four or five different families' rice transplanting: young married women worked on their own husband's and his father's and brothers' land in their marital villages; and also on their own father's and brothers' land in their natal villages. On this occasion, the women of Kalchu's household had been joined by his two sisters, returned from their husband's villages, his brothers' wives and daughters-in-law, and Sauni – all with the implicit understanding that their help would be reciprocated.

Although the monsoon wasn't due to start for several weeks, there'd been five or six isolated rainy days and the countryside was beginning to look green and fresh already. The willow trees along the river bank were spread with leaves as thin and delicate as tissue paper, and the barley in the fields we passed, though thin and immature, had almost reached its full-grown height. Then as we turned a corner and approached the paddy fields the colours turned to winter ones; the length and breadth of the valley, as far as we could see, was bare unplanted earth, and the only reminder of the season was the occasional tiny patch of the brightest, lushest green imaginable – paddy seedlings, now becoming over-densely clustered, due to be transplanted.

We knew we'd come to Kalchu's land when we spotted Sigarup and Śaṅkar wearing multicoloured *topis* and perched on little single-legged stools inserted into the mud at the frayed edge of one of the patches of green. They were leaning forward, reaching into the mud, uprooting seedlings, tying them into bundles and heaping them into a basket. Seeing us coming they stopped what they were doing and turned around, calling out some ribald remark that made the women mutter to themselves and giggle. Sauni, quickest to respond, shouted some comment back and the boys, looking slightly shocked, began to giggle too, rocking back and forth on their flimsy little stools.

Slightly further on we caught sight of Kalchu, working the bulls and plough. He was balancing on a flat board attached to the back of the plough, beating the bulls' rumps with a stick so they sped through the soft mud, flattening and smoothing the surface for the young plants to take root. As he rode across the field the wind billowed out his cotton tunic and a spray of watery mud showered into the air and then splattered to the ground in a trail behind him.

At last, when the land was prepared to his satisfaction, he drove the bulls out of the field, shouting and whistling and brandishing his stick until they heaved their great bodies out of the mud and clambered laboriously over the bank. He left them in the next field, caked in mud, until they were needed again. Meanwhile, Śankar and Sigarup had come over with their baskets of seedlings. Babies had been settled with their elder sisters on the nearest patch of dry ground and young children had happily absorbed themselves playing in the mud. We were ready to start.

At a signal from Kalchu, the two *Damāi* drummers who'd been waiting on the path started beating their kettledrums. The sound rolled, steady as a heartbeat, over the fields, and everybody looked at Chola, the eldest woman in the household. She smirked, knowing what was expected of her, proud of her status and position. Kalchu handed her one of the bundles of seedlings, and with all eyes watching her, she hitched up her skirt, tucking the surplus material into her waistband, and waded out to the centre of the field, her bare feet leaving deep depressions that the loose mud slowly filled. When she approached the centre, she turned around, seeking advice as to where to begin, and laughing and pointing, everyone told her to move to the left a bit, then to the right. Finally, with all our consent, she bent down and planted a cross of seedlings. In its centre she staked a forked twig on top of which she tied a red cloth streamer, to bless and protect the crop that was about to be planted.

Afterwards, Sauni, Mina and all the other women hitched up their skirts to their knees and stepped off the bank into the mud. Seconds later they were bending over in line, facing the edge of the field, moving slowly backwards into the open as, row upon row, they covered the ground. Each seedling had to be separated from the bunch so it lay flat against two extended fingers. The fingers were then dipped into the ground and removed, leaving the delicate seedlings, wilted and battered, to pick themselves up out of the mud. At first I worked on the end of the line, but time after time, I lagged behind as the line moved on, each woman dextrously flicking the plants from one hand to the other and into the ground, as she covered the area round her. In the end I joined Kāli and a line of young girls, planting at the opposite end of the field, out of the way and at a novice's pace.

The sun on our backs as we bent down was hot and unswerving; but the mud felt cool, and the occasional breeze that stirred through the watery valley, cleaving our loose wet skirts to our thighs, set us suddenly shivering. Kalchu, Sigarup and Śaṅkar kept watch from the banks as we worked, pacing up and down to check on our progress. Sometimes they'd criticize one of the women for planting too thinly or thickly; but most of the time their eyes were on bundles of seedlings that needed replacing. As each woman ran out she'd wave her arms in the air and call out to attract attention, and whichever one of the men noticed her first would hurl another green bundle over the field in her direction. If she was lucky she caught it. More often, as a joke, it came too hard or too high and landed with a calculated splat that bespeckled the woman with mud, and left her protesting about the filthy state of her skirt, her face or her hair.

After several hours the line of women met up with the young girls who were planting in the opposite direction. Most of them straightened up and stretched and then looked around, re-orienting themselves; one or two carried on working, retracing the young girls' steps, moving carefully among the fast-wilting seedlings, as they filled out sparsely-planted patches and covered the ground right up to the banks in the corners. Then with one field – the biggest – completed, we made our way over to the dry ground on the other side of the path for something to eat. As a treat Chola had prepared thick buckwheat pancakes and fried potatoes, and the whole party of about fifty people, including the children, relaxed in the grass and enjoyed the picnic.

After we'd rested and eaten we started on the second field. The drumbeat was still resounding distantly across the valley from someone else's land, where the planting had also begun today. Throughout the morning the drummers had made their way back and forwards on the dry paths between different families' fields, and the sound had been loud and then dim; dominant in our consciousness, then receding to the backs of our minds. Now that I had had some practice I rejoined Sauni and Mina in the line of

201

women, and there was a feeling of companionship as we moved together, joggling hands and elbows as we planted, telling anecdotes and jokes beneath our breath, and cursing Kalchu for his careless criticisms. With our bodies bent, our faces hidden, we occupied a private world that, for all their staring, no one else could penetrate. Sometimes, looking down at the ground, you didn't see the mud and the seedlings you were planting, you tuned instead into the crinkled reflections of other women's faces, their silver necklaces and brightly coloured skirts and, behind these, scudding clouds and the glistening light of the sun. Every now and then one or other of the women would nudge her neighbour and the two of them would giggle and burst into one of the local rice-transplanting songs. After the first few words the rest of the line would usually join in, often laughing more than they were singing:

> The grass is green on the mountains,
> The flowers in bloom by the stream,
> The honey-bee has swarmed in a frenzy
> And the season of plenty is here.

That night, as was the custom during the rice transplanting, all the women who'd worked on Kalchu's land were treated to a meal of rice. Chola had cooked a huge panful in the morning, so by evening it was only very slightly warm, but the gravy she prepared when she'd returned from the fields and lit a fire was fresh and hot. For everyone meals of rice were a special treat indulged in only on celebratory occasions. And however strictly the rice supply was rationed, it never seemed to last throughout the year; there were always embarrassing incidents, times when honoured visitors were offered boiled millet or *rotis* instead of rice and had to put on a show of savouring their food, while inwardly they were choking on the insult. So that night, feeling special and indulged, the women enjoyed their meal. Afterwards most of them stayed awake, talking and laughing and telling stories until the early hours of the morning.

At some time during the evening Sauni heard the dogs barking, announcing the arrival of strangers in the village. Without saying a word and without any comment being passed on her, she got up and left the roomful of women. Standing outside in the quiet of the night she heard, as she had known she would, the sound of young men's voices and their soft urgent whistling. She hurried down the ladder and made her way over to the place on the path where she thought the voices had come from; but there was no one there. Then, casting her eyes around in the darkness, she saw them, hidden by the shadows of the woodpile. Apart from Channa Lāl, her lover, there were five or six men, all from Chaura and from Chhuma; and as soon as Sauni had joined them other young girls and women suddenly appeared, as if from nowhere, their faces only barely visible among layers of folded cotton shawls.

When everyone expected had arrived they made their way over to a place on the back path and then down towards the water-mills. It was a clear night. The moon was almost full; the stars as eye-catching as violets on a leafy woodland path. Stooping down in single file they passed through the low doorway into one of the stone mills. Inside, apart from the pool of light by the entrance, it was as dark as a cave, and the insidious churning of water as it rushed down the chute and under the building drowned out all sounds of the outside world.

During the course of the evening other young boys and girls joined them. They went outside where the summer night-air was as smooth and warm as fresh cow's milk, after the cold damp mill. Linking arms in a circle, boys on one side, girls on the other, they passed long hours of the night singing traditional love songs, swaying gently together in time to the slow lilting rhythm.

When dawn eventually came, Sauni parted from her lover and hurried back to the house, ready for work.

All that day the paddy fields seemed an endless expanse of water: clear cold water that coursed freely through the deep irrigation channels; little trickles that overflowed or leaked through mud banks that needed repairing; still warm water that dully reflected the sky. And as the sun rose overhead, everything glistened and shone: silver coin necklaces, black hair, freshly oiled; bunches of paddy as green as the moss that spreads over beech trunks during the rains. Later on, moving about became a delicate balancing act, a question of creeping lightly along thin mud banks so they didn't collapse, of avoiding falling and crushing the fragile seedlings in the fields on either side.

No one talked to Sauni about her lover, or even asked her where she'd been that night: Mina, Chola, Kāli and most of the other girls and women knew. Kalchu knew too, although he never mentioned it and no one ever mentioned it to him. None of them condoned the betrayal of her husband and his family; and yet they couldn't fail to see the yearning in her heart, and hope, as she did, that one day she and her lover could be together.

For four more days the pattern of the rice transplanting remained the same. In the evenings there was a big rice-meal cooked by Chola. At night, for Sauni and some of the other young girls and women, there were meetings with their lovers, at the water-mills, in someone's stable, at the edge of the forest. And in the daytime – from dawn to dusk – there was planting.

On the fifth and final day the mood in the paddy fields changed. All the women were feeling exhausted; backs, shoulders, legs and heads were aching. The bright skirts and jackets that they'd worn so flamboyantly on the first morning were now covered in mud and as dull as their workaday clothing. Sauni in particular was quiet. Her sense of fun and laughter had gone. She no longer shouted caustic remarks at her brothers, or launched into rice-planting songs and then fell about laughing when she realized that, yet again, she'd garbled the words. Maybe she too was just tired.

Early the following morning she quietly went back to her husband's village. Chola had given her a cloth bag of maize flour to take to his parents – a tacit acknowledgement that her daughter's marriage was a marriage of families and that, for all its sadness, it was a marriage they honoured.

The monsoon started early that year, only a week or so after the paddy had been transplanted. Day after day heavy raindrops pelted the liquid fields. Sometimes it seemed that the tender seedlings were being battered so badly they'd be permanently squashed to the ground; at other times it seemed certain they'd simply be washed away in the flooding. But in time they rose up, sparse green stalks, barely distinguishable between the mud and the grey sheets of mist and rain. And as the monsoon took its course they grew slowly stronger and denser until the whole valley became a sea of luminous green.

During the months that followed there were several festivals when Sauni came home to her *māiti*. Each time, when she first arrived she'd be loud and exuberant – borrowing my soap and shampoo, polishing her jewellery and oiling and plaiting her hair to make herself beautiful. But by the time she was due to go back she'd always be sad. Once I asked her how things were with her lover, and she told me that nothing had changed: there'd been a big meeting between her husband's family and her lover and his family. Huge numbers of men from both of their lineages had gathered on neutral ground – a place by the river midway between their two villages. They'd tried to come to some agreement over adultery money; but nothing had been settled. Her father-in-law had insisted that he wouldn't accept one *suka* less than five thousand rupees; her lover had accused him of being mean and unreasonable. Tempers had become frayed, violence was threatened and the meeting had ended in deadlock.

Some time after the monsoon the irrigation channels were dammed up, cutting off the water supply to the paddy fields, and the soft mud dried as wrinkled and fissured as an old woman's face. The paddy ripened, turning from green, to yellow, to the deep brown of the baked earth. On the day that the harvest was due to begin in October, Chola took an apple and some *puris* to the stone shrine of Bhuiar, the god of the soil. The shrine was a small hut, built on top of a smooth immovable rock in the middle of the village's tract of paddy land. She took the *puris* and the apple inside and left them alongside other families' offerings in gratitude for an abundant crop, virtually unscathed by wind, hail, or pests.

Sauni didn't come back for the harvest. It wasn't a special occasion, as the transplanting had been, and men could work on it as well as women, so there was no real need for outside labour. Again it was a warm sunny day, but this time there were none of the light clouds that preceded the monsoon rains: the sky was as clear and deeply blue as lapis lazuli and, against it, the snow-covered mountain at the end of the valley seemed, all of a sudden, to be brazenly naked. As with the transplanting we worked in a line, each of us gathering a small area of paddy into a cluster, cutting through the base of the stalks with a sickle, and laying the cut sheaf behind us, as we made our way further into the field. Although it required much less skill than the transplanting had done, it was important to cut through the stalks with a single blow. With repeated hacking the ripe grains would have been knocked to the ground and lost in the stubble.

As each field was harvested we gathered up the sheaves and carefully carried them to an area that Kalchu had spread over with rugs and blankets. There, he and Chola beat the sheaves against a heavy stone and the loose grains flew into the air and landed in a pile on the surrounding rugs. Several times during the day Kalchu made the trip back to the house, carrying either the loose grains in a woven sack or the sheaves bound only with rope. He laid the sheaves on the roof in the sun, and several weeks later, when the remaining grains had ripened, he and Śankar threshed them again, this time flailing them with sticks. The grain was then tipped into the heavy wooden chest in the grain storage room, next to the shrine on the upper roof, and the straw was fed to the cattle.

The next time I saw Sauni it was winter. She came home wearing her rope-and-felt snow-shoes. Her face was red from the cold and she sat down, warming her hands by the fire. 'My husband's back,' she said immediately, and it was impossible to tell from her expression what this had meant to her – whether he'd gone crazy and beaten her as she had always feared he would, or even whether he'd decided to take her away with him. Everyone was staring at her, waiting to hear the outcome. 'But he's not staying.' She continued, 'His mother can't stop crying because he says he's made his life in India – building roads.' At that point her ambiguous expression changed; her eyes lit up and her whole face and being radiated happiness. 'He and his father have accepted one thousand rupees. Tomorrow Channa Lāl is coming here, with presents for you all, and taking me home as his wife.'

GLOSSARY

Aula: The southern hills and Terai area of Nepal where the sheep are taken in winter. Literally means malaria or a hot and inhospitable place.

Bāhan: One of many demons that the Maṣṭā gods overcame and transformed into lesser deities. Sometimes referred to as the Maṣṭās' servants.

balṭu: Medicinal herb collected in the mountains for sale in the south.

Bānba: Demon mentioned in a *pareli*.

Ban Bhāi: The god of the forest.

ban chhorāi: The leaving of the forest, a ceremony that used to be held at the end of the season for gathering pine-needles.

ban pasāi: The entering of the forest, the equivalent ceremony at the beginning of the season for gathering pine-needles.

Bāra Bhāi: The Twelve Brothers, a collective name for the Maṣṭā gods. In fact there are many more than twelve.

Bārakot: Region in the southern hills of Nepal.

Bārakote: Person from Bārakot.

baṭuka: Bowl, or type of mushroom shaped like a bowl.

Bhawāni: One of two deities worshipped in the household shrine.

Bhuiar: The god of the soil.

'Bihā bhayo!': 'They're married!'

Bijulī Maṣṭā: One of the Maṣṭā gods.

Chait: Nepāli lunar month, approximately 15 March to 15 April.

Chait Dasaiṅ: Festival associated with Bhawāni in the month of *Chait*.

chang (Tib.): Tibetan rice beer.

chaturdaśi: The day before the full-moon festival.

Chhetri: Hindu caste.

chillim: Cone-shaped clay pipe generally smoked with home-grown tobacco.

chuba (Tib.): Traditional Tibetan coat made of wool or fur.

dāl: Sauce or gravy eaten with rice or *roṭis*.

Damāi: *Ḍum* or Untouchable caste of tailors who are also musicians.

ḍāṅgri: Priest who maintains the shrine and performs animal sacrifices.

dāṅtelo: Thorn bush with magical properties; the berries are used for making oil.

desu: Buckwheat bread that is taken on journeys because it stays fresh for a comparatively long time.

dhāmi: Oracle or spirit medium.

dhamini: Female *dhāmi*.

'dhanyabād': 'Thank you.'

dharamsālā (Also *dharmasālā*): Wayside shelter for travellers. Often built as a religious gesture.

dhoti: Loincloth.

duadaśi: Three days before the full-moon festival.

Ḍum: Male member of an Untouchable caste: *Sārki* – Leather-worker; *Damāi* – Tailor (and musician); *Kāmi* – Blacksmith.

Ḍumini: Female member of an Untouchable caste.

ekādaśi: Eleventh day of the lunar fortnight, four days before the full-moon festival.

gāgro: Large water container.

Ganeś: Hindu god of prosperity with the head of an elephant.

ghaṭ: Cremation site on the river bank.

hātijaro: Medicinal herb sold in the south.

haut: Sweet made by boiling milk until it reduces to a paste.

hirin: Last rites. Usually consists of water being given to the dying by male relatives. Sometimes a coin is placed in the mouth.

'Hiuṅ āyo.': 'It's snowing.'

Indra: The king of the Hindu gods and the god of war. Sometimes said to be the creator or father of the Maṣṭā gods.

iṣṭa: Hereditary ritual trading partner or friend.

jharo: Pitch-pine faggots used for kindling and lighting.

Jimale: Place of village monsoon-settlements.

Kālādika: A grassy plateau close to the village.

Kāmi: *Ḍum* or Untouchable blacksmith caste.

Kānchho: Youngest brother. Here refers to Kalchu's youngest brother. Kalchu's children call him Kānchho Bā, Father's youngest brother.

kankani: Wild vine-like plant of which the shoots, leaves and berries are eaten.

kanyādān: Orthodox Hindu marriage. Literally, Gift of a Virgin.

karaso: Wooden rake.

karāti: Nights leading up to the full-moon festival when the *dhāmis* are possessed and dance.

Kārtik: Nepāli lunar month, approximately 15 October to 15 November.

Kaskā Sundari Devī: Local goddess.

katuka: Medicinal herb sold in the south.

lāḍu: Rice-and-honey ball traditional at weddings.

lekh: Mountain pass.

linga: Pine poll erected outside shrine.

lukal: Leather and wool saddle-bags carried by sheep and goats.

Māilo: Middle brother. Here refers to the brother who is younger than Kalchu but older than Kānchho, the youngest.

māiti: Married woman's natal home and family.

Maiyu: One of two deities worshipped in the household shrine.

mal: Pine-needle and manure fertilizer.

mānā: Quantity of liquid or grain, approximately a pint.

māngal: Traditional song sung at births, weddings and funerals.

mantri: Woman who uses magic incantations to cure illness.

Maṣṭā: The Maṣṭās are the most important gods in the region. They are also referred to as the Bāra Bhāi or the Twelve Brothers.

matawāli: Alcohol-drinking.

mitini: Female ritual friend.

'Mitini āmā ayo.': 'Mother's *mitini* is here.'

pachyauro: Shawl worn by women and often presented on ritual occasions.

paiṭh: Full-moon festival.

pareli: God's life story told through the medium of the possessed *dhāmi*.

pheṭā: Turban worn by men; often a ritual gift.

prasād: Food offered to the gods, eaten in essence, and passed back, blessed, for the people to eat.

puri: Fried unleavened bread.

purnimā: The day of the full moon.

raksi: Alcoholic liquor distilled from barley, millet or rice.

roṭi: Unleavened bread made from wheat, barley, maize or millet flour.

Sārki: Ḍum or Untouchable caste of leatherworkers.

Sāun: Nepāli lunar month, approximately 15 July to 15 August.

Sāun Saṅkrаnti: Festival held on first day of *Sāun*.

sindur: Vermilion powder daubed on bride's hair-parting by her husband. It is also used for *ṭikās*.

suka: Coin with the value of a quarter of a rupee.

tār: Goat-like wild animal that used to be hunted until it was declared an endangered species and its killing was outlawed.

tetradaśi: Two days before the full moon.

tetua: Coarse, handwoven, cotton cloth, brought back from Aula and made into clothes.

ṭikā: Mark of blessing placed on the forehead.

ṭola: Measurement of weight, approximately half an ounce.

ṭopi: Traditional Nepalese cap.

Ṭhakuri: Hindu caste.

Thārpā Bāhan: One of the Bāhan gods.

Ukhāṛi Maṣṭā: One of the Maṣṭā gods.

Viṣnu: One of the main Hindu gods, the god of preservation.

Yāṅgre: One of the Maṣṭā gods.